Youths behaviour, or, Decency in conversation amongst men composed in French by grave persons, for the use and benefit of their youth; with the addition of twenty six new precepts (1663)

Francis Hawkins

Youths behaviour, or, Decency in conversation amongst men composed in French by grave persons, for the use and benefit of their youth ; with the addition of twenty six new precepts
Bienséance de la conversation entre les hommes. English.
Decency in conversation amongst men.
Hawkins, Francis, 1628-1681.
[Edition statement:] The eighth impression, whereunto is added much enlargement of three very usefull and profitable alphabeticall tables, the third table having many hard words added : not untill this year 1663, printed : last of all is added, The first entrance of a youth in the university : all which new additions may be sold by themselves.
Errata: p. [49] at end.
Advertisement: p. [51] at end.
Index: p. [38]-[40].
Added t.p. on p. [41]: New additions unto Youths behaviour, 1650, of some letters.
Translation of Bienséance de la conversation entre les hommes.
[6], 69 [i.e. 67], [51] p.
London : Printed by W. Lee ...,
Wing / Y208
English
Reproduction of the original in the Bodleian Library

Early English Books Online (EEBO) Editions

Imagine holding history in your hands.

Now you can. Digitally preserved and previously accessible only through libraries as Early English Books Online, this rare material is now available in single print editions. Thousands of books written between 1475 and 1700 and ranging from religion to astronomy, medicine to music, can be delivered to your doorstep in individual volumes of high-quality historical reproductions.

We have been compiling these historic treasures for more than 70 years. Long before such a thing as "digital" even existed, ProQuest founder Eugene Power began the noble task of preserving the British Museum's collection on microfilm. He then sought out other rare and endangered titles, providing unparalleled access to these works and collaborating with the world's top academic institutions to make them widely available for the first time. This project furthers that original vision.

These texts have now made the full journey -- from their original printing-press versions available only in rare-book rooms to online library access to new single volumes made possible by the partnership between artifact preservation and modern printing technology. A portion of the proceeds from every book sold supports the libraries and institutions that made this collection possible, and that still work to preserve these invaluable treasures passed down through time.

This is history, traveling through time since the dawn of printing to your own personal library.

Initial Proquest EEBO Print Editions collections include:

Early Literature

This comprehensive collection begins with the famous Elizabethan Era that saw such literary giants as Chaucer, Shakespeare and Marlowe, as well as the introduction of the sonnet. Traveling through Jacobean and Restoration literature, the highlight of this series is the Pollard and Redgrave 1475-1640 selection of the rarest works from the English Renaissance.

Early Documents of World History

This collection combines early English perspectives on world history with documentation of Parliament records, royal decrees and military documents that reveal the delicate balance of Church and State in early English government. For social historians, almanacs and calendars offer insight into daily life of common citizens. This exhaustively complete series presents a thorough picture of history through the English Civil War.

Historical Almanacs

Historically, almanacs served a variety of purposes from the more practical, such as planting and harvesting crops and plotting nautical routes, to predicting the future through the movements of the stars. This collection provides a wide range of consecutive years of "almanacks" and calendars that depict a vast array of everyday life as it was several hundred years ago.

Early History of Astronomy & Space

Humankind has studied the skies for centuries, seeking to find our place in the universe. Some of the most important discoveries in the field of astronomy were made in these texts recorded by ancient stargazers, but almost as impactful were the perspectives of those who considered their discoveries to be heresy. Any independent astronomer will find this an invaluable collection of titles arguing the truth of the cosmic system.

Early History of Industry & Science

Acting as a kind of historical Wall Street, this collection of industry manuals and records explores the thriving industries of construction; textile, especially wool and linen; salt; livestock; and many more.

Early English Wit, Poetry & Satire

The power of literary device was never more in its prime than during this period of history, where a wide array of political and religious satire mocked the status quo and poetry called humankind to transcend the rigors of daily life through love, God or principle. This series comments on historical patterns of the human condition that are still visible today.

Early English Drama & Theatre

This collection needs no introduction, combining the works of some of the greatest canonical writers of all time, including many plays composed for royalty such as Queen Elizabeth I and King Edward VI. In addition, this series includes history and criticism of drama, as well as examinations of technique.

Early History of Travel & Geography

Offering a fascinating view into the perception of the world during the sixteenth and seventeenth centuries, this collection includes accounts of Columbus's discovery of the Americas and encompasses most of the Age of Discovery, during which Europeans and their descendants intensively explored and mapped the world. This series is a wealth of information from some the most groundbreaking explorers.

Early Fables & Fairy Tales

This series includes many translations, some illustrated, of some of the most well-known mythologies of today, including Aesop's Fables and English fairy tales, as well as many Greek, Latin and even Oriental parables and criticism and interpretation on the subject.

Early Documents of Language & Linguistics

The evolution of English and foreign languages is documented in these original texts studying and recording early philology from the study of a variety of languages including Greek, Latin and Chinese, as well as multilingual volumes, to current slang and obscure words. Translations from Latin, Hebrew and Aramaic, grammar treatises and even dictionaries and guides to translation make this collection rich in cultures from around the world.

Early History of the Law

With extensive collections of land tenure and business law "forms" in Great Britain, this is a comprehensive resource for all kinds of early English legal precedents from feudal to constitutional law, Jewish and Jesuit law, laws about public finance to food supply and forestry, and even "immoral conditions." An abundance of law dictionaries, philosophy and history and criticism completes this series.

Early History of Kings, Queens and Royalty

This collection includes debates on the divine right of kings, royal statutes and proclamations, and political ballads and songs as related to a number of English kings and queens, with notable concentrations on foreign rulers King Louis IX and King Louis XIV of France, and King Philip II of Spain. Writings on ancient rulers and royal tradition focus on Scottish and Roman kings, Cleopatra and the Biblical kings Nebuchadnezzar and Solomon.

Early History of Love, Marriage & Sex

Human relationships intrigued and baffled thinkers and writers well before the postmodern age of psychology and self-help. Now readers can access the insights and intricacies of Anglo-Saxon interactions in sex and love, marriage and politics, and the truth that lies somewhere in between action and thought.

Early History of Medicine, Health & Disease

This series includes fascinating studies on the human brain from as early as the 16th century, as well as early studies on the physiological effects of tobacco use. Anatomy texts, medical treatises and wound treatment are also discussed, revealing the exponential development of medical theory and practice over more than two hundred years.

Early History of Logic, Science and Math

The "hard sciences" developed exponentially during the 16th and 17th centuries, both relying upon centuries of tradition and adding to the foundation of modern application, as is evidenced by this extensive collection. This is a rich collection of practical mathematics as applied to business, carpentry and geography as well as explorations of mathematical instruments and arithmetic; logic and logicians such as Aristotle and Socrates; and a number of scientific disciplines from natural history to physics.

Early History of Military, War and Weaponry

Any professional or amateur student of war will thrill at the untold riches in this collection of war theory and practice in the early Western World. The Age of Discovery and Enlightenment was also a time of great political and religious unrest, revealed in accounts of conflicts such as the Wars of the Roses.

Early History of Food

This collection combines the commercial aspects of food handling, preservation and supply to the more specific aspects of canning and preserving, meat carving, brewing beer and even candy-making with fruits and flowers, with a large resource of cookery and recipe books. Not to be forgotten is a "the great eater of Kent," a study in food habits.

Early History of Religion

From the beginning of recorded history we have looked to the heavens for inspiration and guidance. In these early religious documents, sermons, and pamphlets, we see the spiritual impact on the lives of both royalty and the commoner. We also get insights into a clergy that was growing ever more powerful as a political force. This is one of the world's largest collections of religious works of this type, revealing much about our interpretation of the modern church and spirituality.

Early Social Customs

Social customs, human interaction and leisure are the driving force of any culture. These unique and quirky works give us a glimpse of interesting aspects of day-to-day life as it existed in an earlier time. With books on games, sports, traditions, festivals, and hobbies it is one of the most fascinating collections in the series.

bibliolife
old books. new life.

The BiblioLife Network

This project was made possible in part by the BiblioLife Network (BLN), a project aimed at addressing some of the huge challenges facing book preservationists around the world. The BLN includes libraries, library networks, archives, subject matter experts, online communities and library service providers. We believe every book ever published should be available as a high-quality print reproduction; printed on-demand anywhere in the world. This insures the ongoing accessibility of the content and helps generate sustainable revenue for the libraries and organizations that work to preserve these important materials.

The following book is in the "public domain" and represents an authentic reproduction of the text as printed by the original publisher. While we have attempted to accurately maintain the integrity of the original work, there are sometimes problems with the original work or the micro-film from which the books were digitized. This can result in minor errors in reproduction. Possible imperfections include missing and blurred pages, poor pictures, markings and other reproduction issues beyond our control. Because this work is culturally important, we have made it available as part of our commitment to protecting, preserving, and promoting the world's literature.

GUIDE TO FOLD-OUTS MAPS and OVERSIZED IMAGES

The book you are reading was digitized from microfilm captured over the past thirty to forty years. Years after the creation of the original microfilm, the book was converted to digital files and made available in an online database.

In an online database, page images do not need to conform to the size restrictions found in a printed book. When converting these images back into a printed bound book, the page sizes are standardized in ways that maintain the detail of the original. For large images, such as fold-out maps, the original page image is split into two or more pages

Guidelines used to determine how to split the page image follows:

- Some images are split vertically; large images require vertical and horizontal splits.
- For horizontal splits, the content is split left to right.
- For vertical splits, the content is split from top to bottom.
- For both vertical and horizontal splits, the image is processed from top left to bottom right.

Youths Behaviour,
OR
Decency in Conversation Amongst Men.

Composed in French by Grave Persons, for the use and benefit of their YOUTH.

Now newly turned into English, By

FRANCIS HAWKINS.

Nephew to Sr *Thomas Hawkins*, Translator of *Caussin*'s Holy Court.

With the addition of Twenty six new Precepts, written by a grave Author, which are marked thus (*) and some more Additions,

---

The Eighth IMPRESSION.

Whereunto is added much Enlargement of three very usefull and profitable Alphabeticall Tables: the third Table having many hard words added, not untill this year 1663. Printed.

Last of all is added, The first Entrance of a Youth in the University. All which new Additions may be sold by themselves.

London, Printed for *W. Lee*, and are to be sold at the *Turks-head* in *Fleetstreet* over against *Fetter*-Lane. 1663.

Gentle Youth.
Think it not amiss to Peruse

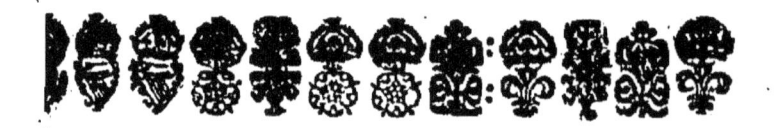

To the Reader.

Gentle Youth,

THink it not amiss to peruse this Piece, yet connive at the style; for it hath need thereof, since wrought by an uncouth and rough file, of [o]ne in green yeares; as being aged under [e]ight. Hence, worthy Reader, shew not thy [se]lf too rigid a Censurer.

This his version is a little disguised, and [th]erefore likely will it appear to thee much [im]perfect. It ought to be his own, or why [u]nder the Title is his Name written? Perad[v]enture thou wilt say, what is it to me? yet [h]ear: Such is it really, as that I presume the [a]uthor may therein be clearly seen to be ren[d]ered faithfully; with this courteously be [y]ou satisfied.

This small Treatise in its use, will evi[d]ently appear to redound to the singular be[n]efit of many a young spirit, to whom solely [a]nd purposely it is addressed. Pass it there[fo]re candidly and without mistake.

In laudem Authoris.

Though here be wonder when 'tis known,
   A child should make this work his own,
(Since he that can translate and please,
Must needs command two languages.)
Yet this is nothing to the rest
Of treasure which this little Chest,
Contains, and will in time bring forth,
To call just Volumes of his worth.
If thus a Branch, what will he be
When he is grown to be a tree?
So glorious in the bud, let men
Look for th' Hesperides agen.
And gather fruit, nor think't unfit
A Child should teach the world more wit.

J. S.

The

The Book-seller to the READER.

ABout Two and twenty years since, at the request of Dr *Hawkins* (the Father of this young Author) I Printed this little Book of *Youths Behaviour*, translated then out of French by his Son. I soon sold that Impression; but being of a small value, I neglected the Printing of it some time; but being desired of many, I Printed a second Impression; which being sold, about seventeen years since, the troubles of War being great, I wholly laid it aside, not intending ever to have Printed the same any more. But some years after, one Mr *Pinchester*, a learned Scholar in *Oxford*, came unto me, desiring me to new Print this little Book, it being, as he said, so excellent a Book to instruct youth in behaviour and good manners, that the like was not extant in any language; further saying, He was going to keep a great School in the City of *Norwich*, and gave me money for Two hundred and fifty of them, which he carried down with him for his Scholars there, to make use of. After that a Counsellor of the middle Temple, in 1652, added twenty five new Precepts marked thus (*) at which time a Gentleman of *Lincolns*-Inn turned the Book

A 4   into

into Latine; and now this year 1662, I have again this eighth time Printed it, with some new Additions of Sayings and Sentences in Latine and English, much in use, to adorn discourse and understanding; as also to encourage in the knowledge and way to understand Latine. As further is added two other Alphabetical Tables, of those words that be used in naming of any Art or Science. The third and last Table is much enlarged, explaining most usuall hard words, used in this Book and others: and at the end of the Precepts is added, *The first Entrance of a Youth in the University.*

I have heard and known so much of the approbation and use of this little Book, for the instructing of both sexes of all ages, that a few lines could not contain the worth and profit therein: notwithstanding there is a Person of great worth is about the writing of the second Part of *Youths Behaviour*, being most applied to the instructing of Women, especially the younger sort of Maids, and Boarders at Schools.

Novemb. 6. 1662.

Yours,

William Lee.

Youths

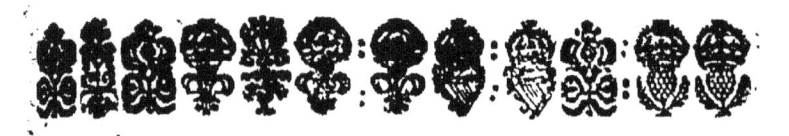

Youths Behaviour,
OR
DECENCIE
In Conversation amongst Men.

CHAPTER I.

General and mixt Precepts as touching Civility among Men.

Every Action done in the view of the world, ought to be accompanied with some sign of reverence, which one beareth to all who are present

2. It is ill-beseeming to put one in mind of any unclean or ill-favoured thing.

3. Take heed as much as thou canst in the presence of others, to put thy hand to any part of thy body, which is not ordinarily discovered; as are the hands and face: and to accustome thy self thereunto, it is well done to abstain from so doing, yea being alone.

4. Do not thou shew any thing to thy companion which may affright him.

5. Sing not within thy mouth, humming to thy self, unless thou be alone, in such sort as thou

thou canst not be heard by others. Strike not up a Drum with thy fingers, or thy feet.

6. Rub not thy teeth nor crash them, nor make any thing crack in such manner that thou disquiet any body.

7. It is an uncivil thing to stretch out thine arms at length, and writhe them hither and thither.

8. In coughing, or sneezing, make not great noise, if it be possible, and send not forth any sigh, in such wise that others observe thee, without great occasion.

9. In yawning howl not, and thou shouldst abstain as much as thou canst to yawn, especially when thou speakest, for that sheweth one to be weary, and that one little accounted of the company: but if thou beest constrained to yawn, by all means, for that time being, speak not, nor gape wide mouthed, but shut thy mouth with thy hand, or with thy handkerchief if it be needfull, readily turning thy face to another side.

10. When thou blowest thy Nose, make not thy Nose sound like a Trumpet, and after look not within thy handkerchief. Take heed thou blow not thy Nose as children do, with their fingers, or their sleeves, but serve thy self of thy handkerchief.

11. To sleep when others speak, to sit when others stand, to walk on when others stay, to speak when one should hold his peace, or hear

others,

touching Civility among Men. 3

others, are all things of ill manners: but it is permitted to a superiour to walk in certain places, as to a Master in his School.

12. It is a thing unseemly to leave ones bed out of order, and one ought not to put off ones clothes in the presence of others, nor go out of ones Chamber half unready, or with a night-cap. Let not thy chamber nor thy table where thou studiest, be unhandsome, especially in the sight of another, and if so be that thou hast one to make thy bed, leave it not uncovered when thou goest out thence.

13. During the time thou shouldest study, if thou beest in the company of others, it is not fit to make a noise, or read so loud that thou beest understood by others who study: Likewise it is mis-beseeming to study, or read other Books unseasonably, while the Master explicateth a Lesson, as also to hinder thy fellows attentions.

14. Hearing thy Master, or likewise the Preacher, wriggle not thy self, as seeming unable to contain thy self within thy skin, making shew thy self to be the knowing and sufficient person, to the misprice of others.

15. At play, and at fire, good manners will, that one give place to them who are newly come.

16. Take heed that in playing thou do not over-heat thy self; Contest not, nor speak louder than thou maist with moderation. Drink not

not when thou art hot, be it that it cometh by play or by walking apace, or other labour, for it is a thing very prejudiciall to health, to drink at such a time.

17. It is not decent to spit upon the fire, much less to lay hands upon the embers, or to put them into the flame to warm ones self, nor is it beseeming to stoop so low as even to crowching, and as it were one sate on the ground. If there be any meat on the fire, thou oughtest not to set thy foot thereon, to heat it. In the presence of a well-bred company, it is uncomely to turn ones back to the fire, or to approach nigher than others, for the one and the other savoureth of preheminence. It is not permitted but to the chief in quality, or to him who hath charge of the fire, to stir up the fire with the fire-fork, or to kindle it, take it away, or put fuel on it.

18. When thou sittest, put not undecently one leg upon the other, but keep them firm and setled: and joyn thy feet even, cross them not one upon the other.

19. Gnaw not thy nails in the presence of others, nor bite them with thy teeth.

20. Spit not on thy fingers, and draw them not as if it were to make them longer: also snifle not in the sight of others.

21. Neither shake thy head, feet, or legs; Rowl not thine eyes. Lift not one of thine eye-brows higher than thine other. Wry not

not thy mouth. Take heed that with thy spittle thou bedew not his face with whom thou speakest, and to that end approach not too nigh him.

22. Kill not a Flea or other unclean Vermine in the presence of others; And if thou seest any filth on the ground, as some thick spittle or the like, put thy foot thereon dexterously if thou canst: if that were upon the clothes of thy companion, shew it not to others, but if thou canst put it off neatly, yet without his taking notice thereof, if it may so be; and if another do for thee the like office, shew thy self unto him with tender of thanks.

23. Spit not far off thee, nor behind thee, but aside, a little distant and not right before thy companion: but if it be some gross flegm, one ought if it may be, tread upon it. Be-spit not the windows in the streets, nor spit on the fire, nor on a bason, nor on any place where the spittle cannot be taken away, by putting thy foot thereon.

24. Turn not thy back to others, especially in speaking; Jog not the Table, or Desk, on which another doth read or write; Lean not upon any one; pull not him by his Cloak to speak to him; push him not with thine elbow.

25. Set not in order at every hand while, thy beard or thy stockings. Keep not thy nails foul,

foul, or too long, and keep thy hands and thy teeth clean, yet without over-much attendance thereon, or curiosity.

26. Puff not up thy cheeks; Lall not out thy tongue; Rub not thy beard nor thy hands, Thrust not out thy lips, or bite them, and keep them neither too open, or too shut.

27. Take heed thou beest not a flatterer: for such an one sheweth to have little opinion of the judgement of him whom he flattereth, holding him for a simple fellow. Play not with him, who taketh no pleasure therein.

28. It becometh not to read Letters, Books, or other Writings, whilest one is in company, unless there be some necessity, and as it were in passing by; and then also thou shouldest crave leave of the company, be it not, that thou art the chief of them all. No more maist thou touch the Writings, Books, or such like things of others, nor go near them, nor fix thine eyes upon them, unless thou beest invited thereunto, by him who is the owner of them: and thou shouldest not blame them or praise them, untill one asketh thy advice therein. Also thou oughtest not to approach or look nigh, when another readeth a Letter or such like thing.

29. Let not thy countenance be like that of a phantasticall or hair-brain'd, stern, amazed, melancholick, pensive, inconstant man, in such sort that one thereby may discern some

passion

passion or unruly affection: rather shew a good countenance and pleasant chear, avoiding too much mirth in serious affairs, and too much gravity in things familiar and ordinary.

30. † Let the gestures of thy body, be agreeable to the matter of thy discourse, for it hath been ever held a solœcisme in Oratory, to point to the Earth when thou talkest of Heaven.

31. † Scorn not any for the infirmities of nature, which by no art can be amended, nor do thou delight to put them in mind of them, since it very often procures envy, and promotes malice, even to Revenge.

32. † When thou shalt hear the misfortunes of another, shew not thy self gladded for it, though it hap to thy enemy, for that will argue a mind mischievous, and will convict thee of a desire, to have executed it thy self, had either power or opportunity seconded thy will.

33. † When thou seest justice executed on any, thou maist inwardly take delight in his vigilancy to punish offendors, because it tends to publick quiet, yet shew pity to the offender; and ever constitute the defect of his morality thy precaution.

34. † Laugh not too much or too loud, in any publick spectacle, lest for thy so doing, thou present thy self, the only thing worthy to be laughed at.

CHAP.

CHAP. II.

Of the first Duties and Ceremonies in Conversation.

Although superfluous Complements, and all affectation in Ceremonies are to be eschewed, yet thou oughtest not to leave them which are due, otherwise thou displeasest the person with whom thou dost converse.

2. Put off thy Cap or Hat, to persons of desert, as are Church-men, Justices, and the like, turning the Cap or Hat to thy self-wards, make them a reverence, bowing thy self more or less, according to the quality of the persons, and the custome of the better-bred. So in like sort it is an undecent thing, not to do reverence to whom it appertaineth, and among thy equals, to expect that thy companion prevent thee in that duty. Also to put off ones Hat when there is no necessity, appeareth to have of affectation; in like manner it is reproveable, to observe whether one doth re-salute thee: for the rest in manner of saluting, or re-saluting by word, keep the most common custome of the best-trained up.

3. It is ill said, Sir, be covered, or put on your Hat, to one of more eminency than thy self, as also not to say so much, to whom it is due. Likewise he who maketh too much hast, to put on his Hat, and he who at the first putteth

th not on, or after some few intreaties, do not well: and therefore one ought to be covered after the first, or for the most part after the second time; if so that in some Countries the Countrey custom be not received, and amongst equals, or superiours, who are of the self-same house, the inferiour may cover himself at the first request. True it is, that equals at the instant, or immediately after, are wont to enterchange a sign of covering themselves joyntly. Now what herein is spoken of qualification in behaviour, ought likewise to be conceived, in what concerneth taking of place and sitting down: for Ceremonies without bounds are too troublesome.

4. He who being inferiour, or held for such an one, would put on his hat, his companion being uncovered, ought to demand leave of the other: then in good time let him do so; upon condition, that he may presume that nothing will offend the other.

5. If any one come to speak with thee whilst thou sittest; stand up, especially if the person do merit it, be it that he be greater than thy self: or for that he is not thy familiar, or though for the rest he were thy equal, or thy inferiour: and if there be any thing for one to sit on, be it a chair, be it a stool, give to each one his due.

6. When thou shalt meet any one of greater rank than thy self, thou oughtest to stay thy self, yea, and even retire a little; especially if

the meeting be at a door, or other straight passage, giving way that he may pass.

7. Walking in company of the like, thou shalt give them the more worthy hand (according to the custome of the Countrey,) in which speaking in general, it seemeth to be the most common use, that the more noble place is on the right hand, the right, I say, in such sort, that he who doth honour to any other, placing himself on his left hand giveth him the right. But if three walk together, the chiefest place in rank is for the most part, that of the middest; then that which is on the right hand, and the last that of the left. Yet in *France*, for so much as the place near the wall is ordinarily more high, more sure, for easie walking, and cleaner, commonly one giveth it to the more worthy, namely, where there are but two

8. Being with thy equals, be not the first to take the best place: but if one present it unto thee, be not wilfull in refusing it: thou maist well express some act of civil courtesie, shewing that thou acceptest it rather to obey them, or for that thou wouldest not enter into importunate striving, than for any merit of thine; at least let it appear, that thou rendrest thanks.

9. If any one far surpassing others, either in age or desert, would give place to a meaner than himself in his own lodging, or elsewhere; even as he ought not to accept of it, so he on the

the other part should not use much earnest-
ness, nor offer it unto him more than once or
twice; to the end he be not suspected of inci-
vility.

10. But to him who is ones peer, or almost
the same, one ought to give the chiefest place
in ones own lodging, and he ought gently to
refuse it, then at the second offer to accept it,
with thanksgiving and recognizance.

11. In walking to and fro an house, thou
oughtest to observe the same, but it is enough
that one puts ones self at the left hand at the
first, and afterwards continue where one is.
Which may likewise be observed, being with
ones superiours; yet use the most common
custome of the Countrey

12. They who are in dignity, or in office,
have precedence in all places: but whilest they
are young, they ought, to respect them who
are their equals in birth, or other qualities, although they have not any publick charge, if
they be much more aged, principally if
they have the degree of Doctorship: nay,
when they give to them the chiefest place,
they ought notwithstanding at the first to
refuse it, afterwards to take it civilly with
thanksgiving.

13. It is good manners to prefer them to
whom one speaketh, before ones self, especially if they be far above us, with whom in no
sort one ought to commence.

B 2   14. Meeting

14. Meeting by the way the Chief Magistrates of the City, or other persons of like quality, it is the duty of each one to do them the reverence which appertaineth to them, staying ones self untill they be passed by.

15. For that which concerneth Ceremonies, or Complements, we ought to have respect of time, place, age, and condition of persons: and with them who are much employed, we must be brief, nay, rather we should make them understand by sign, that which we would say unto them.

16. Even as Artificers, and other persons of low conditions, ought not to trouble themselves to use many ceremonies to them who are great, and Lords; but respect them, and humbly honour them; so likewise on the other part they ought to treat with them in all sort of affability and courtesie, keeing themselves from each action, or sin of arrogancy.

17 Speaking to men of quality, lean not, and look them not wishly in the face, approach not too near them, and at the least they keep self a pace from them, or there-about.

18. Visiting any sick body do not play suddenly the Doctor of Physicks part, if thou therein understand nothing.

19. Writing Letters, or speaking to any person of honour and quality, thou shalt give to each one the title which belongeth to him, answerable to his degree, and the custom of the
Countrey:

ountry: and it will not be to ill purpose to
ad over again that which thou hast written,
the end, thou maist correct the faults, if any
erein be found.

20. Strive not with thy Superiours in argu-
ent or discourse; but always submit thy opi-
ion to their riper judgments, with modesty;
nce the possibility of erring, doth rather ac-
mpany green than gray hairs.

21. † Do not undertake to teach thy equal,
the Art himself professeth; for that will sa-
ur of Arrogancy, and serve for little other
an to brand thy judgment with Rashness.

22. † Let thy Ceremonies in courtesie be
oper to the dignity and place of him with
hom thou conversest: for it is absurd to hour a Clown with words courtly and of mag-
ficence.

23. † Do not thou express joy before one
k, or in pain: for that contrary passion, will
sily aggravate his misery. Do thou rather
mpathize his infirmities: for that will af-
ard a gratefull easement, by a seeming parti-
ation.

24. † Shew thy self humble, tractable, to thy
periours, especially to Magistrates, and men
Authority; let thy demeanour towards thy
uals be such as may argue thee free from ar-
gancy; And be thou assured that gentle af-
ility towards thy inferiours, will fix to thy
me the Epithite of courteous.

CHAP.

CHAP. III.

Of the fashions of qualifying, or titling of Persons to whom one speaketh, to advise them to break a jest

TOuching the Titles and Attributes which commonly one giveth to great persons, it is needfull to observe the use of times, and of the Countrey, and to take counsell of them who are versed and experienced in such things. Also one ought to take heed in speaking to such an one, that one change not his title, giving unto him sometimes one, sometimes another, if one be not mistaken at the first.

2. To persons of lesser rank, one saith, *You*, without thou-ing any body, be it not some little child, and that thou wert much more aged, and that the custome it self amongst the meer courteous and better bred, were to speak in such manner. Yet, Fathers to their Children, untill a certain age, as in *France* untill they be set at liberty; Masters to their little Scholars, and others of like command, seem according to the more common use, to have power to say, *Thou*, *Thee*, even plainly: for, what concerneth familiar friends, amongst them the custome doth comport in certain places, that they (*Thou*) one another more freely, in other places one's more reserved.

3. When a man doth the uttermost he can, and ought, although it succeedeth not

for titling of Perſons.

thy wiſhes, take heed to blame him, for he rather deſerveth praiſe.

4. Having whereof to adviſe or reprehend any one, take good heed whether it ought to be done in publick, or private, or indeed whether it be fit to remit it to another time: conſider in what terms thou ſhouldeſt do it; eſpecially when he ſhould be counſelled, ſeem not to give hope of remedy to his paſſed, or future faults: above all, in reproving any one ſhew no ſign of choler, nor ſpeak to him with ſo high an accent but do it with all ſweetnes.

5. Being admoniſhed of any whoſoever, and what time, and place ſoever, ſhew to take it good part, thanking him who hath done thee ſuch an office; but afterwards being not culpable, it ſeem to thee neceſſary to juſtifie thy ſelf, thou maiſt do it in time, and place, and with decency, rather to content him who adviſeth thee, than to excuſe thy ſelf, eſpecially if he be thy ſuperiour.

6. Reproach not any mans imperfections, though they be natural. Take not pleaſure to make any body bluſh, either by thy deed or word.

7. Neither mock nor ſcoff in any thing of importance, nor be reproachful, nor alſo break a jeſt, biting like a dog; but if thou delivereſt any conceit which is ready, and not too much premeditated, and without offence to any body, thou maiſt do well; witty conceits and paſ-

B 4 ſages

sages of the tongue, ought not to be in base and misbeseeming things, such as are those of Jesters; and when it so falleth out, that thou deliver some happy, lively, and jolly conceit, abstain thou, and let others laugh.

8. † Be sure thy conversation be in that point vertuous, wherein thou art desirous to retain another, lest thy actions render thy advice unprofitable; since the ratification of any advice, is the serious prosecution of that vertue, for example hath ever been more prevalent than precept.

9. † In writing or speaking to any, deprive them not of their acquired title, lest thou seem Censorious of their deserts.

10. † Thou oughtest not too suddenly to believe a flying Rumour of a friend, or any other, but let charity guide thy judgment untill more certainty, for by this means thou securest his Reputation, and freest thy self of rashness.

11. † Use no reproachfull language against any man, nor curse, nor revile, for improperations and imprecations will rather betray thy affections to censure, than in any manner hurt him against whom thou utterest them.

CHAP. IV.

Of Clothes and Arraying the Body.

BE not too solicitous in setting thy bands, thy hair, or thy beard; carry not about thee

for Arraying the Body.   17

any sweet smell, wear not thy hat too high on thy head, nor too close on thine eyes, not in the fashion of swaggerers and jesters.

2. Untruss not thy self, nor make thy self ready for the close-stool in the presence of others; afterwards if thou be to touch any meat, &c, wash thine hands, but if it may be, not in the sight of any whosoever.

3. It is a point of cleanliness, and of wholsomness, to wash ones hands and face as soon as one is up, and to comb ones head in time and season, yet not too curiously.

4. Wear not thy clothes foul, unsewed, dusty, nor old; look that they be brushed commonly once a day; take heed where thou sittest or kneelest, and whom thou approachest, for fear that there be dust or some uncleanness; carry not thy Cloke under thine arm like a Braggadoche; if thou layest by thy Cloke, or thy Gown, wrap it up, taking heed where thou puttest it.

5. For what concerneth Clothes, accommodate thy self to the fashion of thy equals, civill and orderly men, according to the use of times and places. Yet thy Clothes ought to be rather more plain and grave, regard had to others, than richer and better.

6. † Ever be modest in thy apparel, rather seeking to accommodate Nature, than curious by Art to procure admiration: Clothes may give thee ornament, but the judicious will never

ver seek thy perfection on thy out-side, and I'm sure if decency be thy only aim, thou wilt be sure to shoulder off the censure of a phantastick.

7. † Admire not thy self in thy apparel, for that will so far demonstrate thy defects, as thou art willing to seek perfection in the skill of a Tailor.

CHAP. V.

Of walking, be it alone, or in Company.

RUn not in the streets, also go not too slowly, nor with thy mouth open. Move not to and fro in walking, go not like a Ninny, nor hang thy hands downwards, shake not thine arms, kick not the earth with thy feet, throw not thy legs a-cross here and there, and walking drail not thy feet after thee, truss not up thy breeches at every hand while, go not upon the top of thy toes, nor in a dancing fashion, nor in a stooping, nor in a capering, or in a tripping manner with thy heels.

2. Play not the Peacock, looking every where about thee, whether thou beest well decked and trim, if thy shoes fit well, if thy stockings be fitly drawn up, and thy other clothes handsome, and well accommodated. Go not out of thy chamber with thy pen in thine ear, cap, or hat; carry not thy handkerchief in thy hand, nor in thy mouth, nor hang it

for walking in Company.

thy girdle, nor under thine arm, nor upon
shoulders, nor under thy Gown; but put it
place where others see it not, and from
nce thou maist take it out when thou
left. Beware although thou hadst scarcely
le use thereof, to present it to others.

. Eat not in the streets, principally in the
vn, beest thou alone, nor in company; nor
e house out of season, and in the presence
rangers.

. Laugh not, nor speak not, thou being
e; for it is not the part of a man. Walking
e, sing not in such manner that thou be
r-heard. Make not any sign of admirati-
as if thou thoughtest of some great busi-
; Also throw not in the streets stones nor
ks, or any other thing. Tread not purpose-
n the pebble stones, and remove them not
of their places, for it is the act of a fool.
net with thy head too high, nor too low,
hanging to the right, or left, and look not
dily here and there.

;. Above all things, if thou esteemest of thy
utation, associate thy self with men of good
lity; but if it cannot be, because thou
west none, or for some other reason, it
re better as one saith, to be alone, than ill
ompanied.

5. If thou goest with one of thy rank, take
the upper hand, and amuse not on point
precedence, and having not the place
which

which belongeth to thee, let it not trouble thee, but go on roundly. If in dignity he be more eminent than thou art, give him the right hand, or the most worthy place, and beware thou go not before him.

7. Walking up and down an house with one only, if he be greater than thy self, at first give him the right hand, and stop thou not then, when he stayeth, be not the first to return, and turn not thy back to him, but thy self towards him. If he be a man of great quality, walk not at all with him cheek by joul, but some-what behind him; yet in such manner, that he may easily speak to thee. If he be thy equal, carry thy self so, that thou turn proportionably with him, and make him not always the first: Likewise stop not too often at mid-way, if there be not great necessity, for that favoureth of superiority, and is accounted troublesome. He in the middest walking with equals, or as it were equals, ought to turn himself, now to the right, then to the left hand; and if so be that they be not equals, let him turn for the most part towards him who deserveth best. Finally, they who are on the side, ought always to turn themselves towards him who is the mid'st, neither before him nor behind him.

8. † In thy walkings alone, express no passion in thy gesture, lest by that means thou shouldest turn thy brest into Christal, and let others read thy mind at a distance.

CHAP.

CHAP. VI.
Of Discourse.

† Let thy conversation be without malice or envy, for that is a sign of a tra[ct]able and commendable nature; And in all [iss]ues of passion, admit reason for thy gover[nes]s, so shall thy reputation be either altoge[th]er inviolable, or at the least not stained with [co]mmon Tinctures.

2. † Never express any thing un-beseem[ing], nor act against the Rules Moral before thy [inf]eriours, for in these things thine own guilt [wi]ll multiply crimes by example, and as it [we]re, confirm ill by authority.

3. † Be not immodest in urging thy friend to [dis]cover his secrets; lest an accidental discove[ry] of them work a breach in your amity.

4. Utter not frivolous things amongst grave [and] learned men, nor any very difficult questi[on] or subject amongst the ignorant, nor things [wh]ich are hard to be believed. Farce not thy [lan]guage with Sentences, especially amongst [thi]ne equals, and much less amongst thy bet[ter]s : Speak not of mischances, and dolefull [thi]ngs inoportunely, and to the company : [in t]ime of mirth, or at the Table, speak not of [me]lancholick things, of wounds, of sculs of [dea]th; and if others speak in that kind, change [the] discourse if thou canst dexterously. Tell [not] thy dreams, if it be not to thy intimatest
friends,

friends, when they might seem to be of great and notable presage, to which notwithstanding thou shalt not give credit.

5. A man wel bred ought not to vaunt himself of his brave atchievments, or rare qualities of wit, of vertue, or of the like; much less of his nobleness, honour, riches, or his kindred, if he be not more than constrained; also he ought not to depress himself too much without occasion.

6. It is to no purpose to break a jest there, where one taketh no pleasure in mirth; laugh not aloud, and to the disfiguring of thy countenance, or without subject, only by custome; deride not the mis-fortune of any one, although there seem to be some cause why.

7. Speak not an injurious word, be it in jest or in earnest. Nip not any by word; likewise one ought not to scoff any body, especially if they be greater than thy self, although they give occasion.

8. Be not froward but friendly, and courteous, and the first to salute others; hear and answer; and be not pensive when it is a time to converse and discourse.

9. By no means detract from any other, nor speak of things which belong unto him; also be not too excessive in praising.

10. Go not thither where thou knowest not whether thou shalt be welcome. Give not thy advice, except one ask it of thee, be it not that
thou

ou art the best there, principally out of season, and where there is no hope of profiting; and being intreated to deliver what thou thinkest, be brief, and come quickly to the point.

11. If two contend amongst themselves, take not the part of either, if thou beest not compelled: and take heed that thou be not obstinate in thine opinion; in things indifferent, be thou on the part of most of the company, who deliver thereon their opinions.

12. Reprehend not the imperfections of others, for it is the part of Fathers, Masters, and Superiours; thou maist well shew notwithstanding, that they distast thee: likewise maist thou now and then safely give some good counsell in time and place.

13. Stay not to gaze on the marks or blemishes appearing on others, although they be natural, principally if they be in the face; and ask not from whence they come; and that which thou well maist speak in secret to thy friend, deliver not in the presence of others.

14. Speak not in an unknown language, or in what thou knowest not well, be it not in case of necessity to be better understood, but use thine own natural tongue, as men of quality of the Town speak it, not like the mean sort; especially take thou heed to utter words which savour of immodesty, although in secret, or to move mirth. Use not homely and
clownish

clownish words; when things sublime and serious are treated of.

15. Speak not before thou thinkest what thou wouldest deliver, and in the vulgar language; and make not a shew of nimble conceits and clinches; Pronounce not imperfectly, nor hastily bring forth thy words; likewise utter not so slowly that thou trouble the hearers.

16. When another speaketh, take heed that through thee he be not neglected by his auditors; and be attentive, turning not thine eyes here and there, nor busie thy self in ought else. If any drawl forth his words, help him not therein, nor prompt him, be it not that he intreat thee so to do, or that it were in private, or that thou hadst great familiarity with him; likewise interrupt him not, nor answer him, untill he have brought his speech to a period.

17. Being in the mid'st of a discourse, ask not of what one treateth; since that it is a draught of authority; but thou may'st well intreat gently that he proceed, if thou perceivest that for thee he hold his peace. On the contrary, if any one come on a suddain whil'st thou talk'st, especially if he be a person of quality, it is seemly to make a little Epilogue, and brief collection of what thou delivereft, and then afterwards go on with thy discourse.

18. Thou oughtest not to make a face or use any other action of undecency with thy mouth, eyes, or with thine hands, to express

what

what thou wouldst deliver, neither oughte'st thou to hold thy hand behind thy back, either clasped or across, for that favoureth of ones preheminence, but place thine hands before thee one over the other, somewhat under the brest, or under thy girdle: when thou talkest be circumspect how thou carriest thy body, shake not thine head; nor move thine hands much, and hold thy feet still.

19. Whilst thou speakest, put not on thy hat, nor ought else before thy mouth. Chew not Paper nor other thing, shake not thy head; deal not blows with thy elbows; stand not titter-tatter on one foot; put not one leg overthwart the other.

20. Point not with thy finger at him of whom thou speakest; approach not too nigh his person, much less his face to whom thou talkest.

12. If thou be'st in company, speak not in secret with whomsoever, but refer it to another time, if so be, that thou hast no authority over them.

22. To treat with men in an unfit time, is to do nothing, or rather to anger them with whom thou wouldest speak.

23. Take thou heed that thou make no comparisons, and if any body happen to be praised for some brave act, or virtue, praise not another for the same virtue in his presence, for every comparison is odious.

24. Be not apt to relate news, if thou know-

est not that for the most part they be true. Discoursing of things which thou hast heard, say not, *who told them unto thee*, if thou thinkest no that he will take it well. What hath been tol thee in secret, relate it not to another.

25. Be not tedious in thy speech, readin , discourse; principally when the thing is small importance, or when thou perceivest that the company doth not well like of it.

26. Be not curious to know the affairs o others, and approach not to that side whe one speaketh in secret.

27. Undertake not that which thou canst not perform, but keep thy promise.

28. When thou do'st a message, deliverest a relation or manifestation of a business, endeavour to do it without passion, and with discretion: although it be thou treatest with persons of mean rank or quality.

29. When those that are thy Tutors talk to any body or other, be thou aware to speak, to laugh, or to hearken to them.

30. Take heed to mumble or make a noise within thy teeth.

31. Assure not that which thou knowest not to be true.

32. Being with persons of more quality than thou art thy self, principally if they have power over thee, speak not untill thou art asked, and then stand upright, put off thine hat, and answer in few words, if to be they give
thee

thee not leave to fit or put on thine hat.

33. In difputes which occurre efpecially in converfation, be not fo defirous to winne, that thou leave no liberty to each one to deliver his opinion; and be it that thou art in the wrong, thou ought'ft to give way to the judgment of the major part, or at the leaft to the moft cholerick and peevifh, and far rather to them under whom thou art, or who are judges of the difpute.

34. Although thou be'ft bitten, or injured by words, anfwer not; and endeavour not to defend thy felf; but make fhew to take them in jeft, and that thou careft not for them; although others do move thee to defend thy felf: for as the Proverb faith, *Each quiftion doth not deferve an anfwer.*

35. Contradict not at every hand-while, that which others fay, contending and faying, *It is not fo, it is as I fay*: but reply thy felf thereIn to the opinion of others: principally when the things are of fmall confequence.

36. Being in company alfo even with them of thy condition, play not the Mountebank and pratler, but fpeak with meafure and in due time, having wherewithall to talk to the purpofe of that which is handled, and with certainty of truth: for to fpeak or rehearfe a thing, not knowing it, and afterwards to excufe one felf, in faying, *I do not remember it well, I, I know well, that I have read it*; that becometh not

C 2 34.

37. If any one had begun to rehearse an History, say not, *I know it well*; and if he relate it not aright, and fully, shake not thine head, twinkle not thine eyes, and snigger not thereat; much lesse mayst thou say, *It is not so, you deceive your self.*

38. Speak not very loud, as would the Crier of Proclamations: nor speak so low, that one cannot understand thee.

39. Let thy carriage be beseeming a man, moderately grave, setled and attentive to that which is spoken: to the end, thou hast not occasion to say at every discourse; *What say you? How hapned that? I understand you not*, and the like.

40. In discourses, walking, hold not back thy companion as it were by a bridle, staying him at every three words. Approach not so nigh unto him, that thou justle him. Keep not thy self further from him than a span, or thereabout.

41. Be not a year in the beginning of a discourse, and in certain long excuses, or ceremonies, saying, *Sir, excuse me, if I know not to deliver my self well, &c. yet to obey you, &c.* and other like troublesome and sottish drawlings, and nice curiosities; but enter readily into the matter as much as may be, with moderate boldness, then proceed without being troubled, even to the end. Be not tedious, make not many digressions, nor repeat oftentimes the same manner of speech.

42. He who hath an unready speech, let him not alwayes take upon him the Discourse, but let him endeavour to correct the default of his tongue by silence, and good attention.

43. Speak not evil of one absent, for it is unjust to detract from the worth of any, or besmear a good name by condemning, where the party is not present to clear himsel, or undergo a natural Conviction.

44. † It is a thing very improper, if not altogether ridiculous, to treat of matters above the capacity of thy Auditors, for by so doing, though thou should'st purchase admiration from their ignorance; yet it will procure derision from the wise, since by that means thy discourse will become common air, and they who hear thee, will be altogether unsatisfied in thy Conclusions.

CHAP. VII.

Of Carriage at the Table.

BEing set at the Table, scratch not thy self, and take thou heed as much as thou canst to spit, cough, and to blow at thy nose; but if it be needfull, do it dexterously without much noise, turning thy face sideling.

2. Take not thy repast like a Glutton.

3. Break not bread with thy hands, but cut it with a Knife, if it be not very little, and very new, and that all the others
did

did the same, or the major part.

4. Cast not thy self upon the Table with thine arms stretched even to thy elbows. And lean not thy shouldiers, or thine arms, on thy chair undecently.

5. Eate not with cheeks full, and with full mouth.

6. Sop not in Wine, if thou be'st not the Master of the house, or hast some indisposition or other.

7. Make not shew to take great delight in thy Meat or in thy Wine; but if he who feasteth thee, ask how thou likest it, thou mayst answer him with modesty and prudence; much less should'st thou find fault with the meat, or procure others or more.

8. Taking Salt, beware that thy Knife be not greasie, when it ought to be wiped, or the fork; one may do it neatly with a little piece of bread, or as in certain places with a Napkin, but never with a whole loaf.

9. Entertaining any one, it is decent to serve him at the Table, and present him with meats, yea, even those which are nigh him; but if one be invited by another, it is better to attend untill that the Master or other do carve him meat, than that he take it himself, were it not that the Master intreat him to take it freely, or that one were in house of a familiar friend. Also one ought scarce offer ones self, as undesired to serve others out of ones house, where
one

one might have little power, be it not that the number of the guests were great, and that the Master of the house could not have an eye to all the company, then one may crave to them who are near ones self.

10. Blow not upon thy meat, but if it be hot stay untill it be cold; broath may be cooled, turning it gently with a spoon, but it is not comely to sup ones broath at Table, it ought to be eaten with a spoon.

11. Smell not to thy meat, and if thou holdest thy nose to it, set it not afterwards before another.

12. Besmear not any bread round about with thy fingers, but when thou wilt cut some bread, wipe them first if they be greasie; Therefore take heed as nigh as thou canst, of souling thy hands or of greazing thy fingers, and having a spoon or fork, make use of it, it becometh thee, according to the custom of the best bred.

13. If thou soakest thy bread or meat in the sauce, soak it not again, after that thou hast bitten it, dip therein at each time a reasonable morsel, which may be eaten at one mouthfull.

14. One ought not to cast under the Table, or on the ground, bones, parings, wine or such like things; notwithstanding if one be constrained to spit something which was hard to chew, or which causeth irksomness, then may one throw it dext'rously forth upon the ground, taking it decently with two fingers, or with

with the left hand half shut, so that it be not a liquid thing, in such case one may more freely spit it on the ground, turning ones self if it be possible somewhat aside, as hath been said here above.

15. Likewise it appeareth not a seemly thing, to spit forth the stones of Plums, Cherries, or such like on a dish, but one ought first to gather them neatly, as it hath been said, in the left hand, bearing it to ones mouth, and then lay them upon the brim of a trencher.

16. Put not thy meat in thy mouth, holding thy knife in thy hands, as do the Countrey Clowns.

17. Cast not thine eys upon the trenchers of others, and fix them not wishfully upon the meat on the Table, and lift them not up whilst thou drinkest, or whilst thou puttest the meat in thy mouth.

18. Cut not too much bread at once, and make not too great shives, but of a small or middle size. Cut thy bread even, without framing a Tub thereof, take unto thee only the crumb thereof, also flaw it not, solely taking the crust thereof; cut not morsels of bread upon thy trencher.

19. If thou hast bad teeth, in such manner that thou canst not eat a crust of bread, or bread burned, or too hard, it seemeth better to pare the piece thou cuttest, than the whole loaf.

20. It

for Carriage at the Table.

20. It is mis-beseeming to stoop much to ones dish, or meat; it sufficeth to bow a little then when one carrieth the morsel which is sauced to ones mouth, to the end, that one foul not ones self, and afterwards to sit upright again.

21. One ought sometimes to look off the meat, yet without gazing to and fro, or wishly looking upon the guests, or them who wait, or on the meat which is before others.

22. In like manner it is undecent to soil the Table cloath; and that which is worse, to clean ones face, or wipe away ones sweat with the Napkin, or with the same clean ones nose, ones trencher, or the dish.

23. Present not to others that whereof thou hast first tasted, be it wine or other thing.

24. Wipe not thy hands on thy bread when they are foul, nor on the Table-cloath, but on the end of thy Napkin, and take heed thou dost not foul it all over, and so thou be'st counted a sloven after dinner.

25. When thou eatest or drinkest, make not much noise with thy teeth, neither in supping, nor in grinding too hard, nor in any other manner.

26. Suck no bones, at least in such wise, that one may hear it; take them not with two hands, but with one solely and properly. Gnaw them not, nor tear the flesh with thy teeth, as Dogs do; but make use of thy Knife, holding
them

them with one hand, or rather with two fingers, as nigh as thou canst. Knock no bones upon thy bread, or trencher, to get out the marrow of them, but get out the marrow with a knife; to speak better, it is the consel of the most wise, that it is not fit to handle bones, and much less to mouth them.

27. Make not use of a knife to break bones, Plum-stones, or other hard thing; also break them not with thy teeth, or other thing, but let them alone.

28. Take not from the common dish, that which is before thy companion, but only that which is on thy side, and also no more than others; and if they be fruits, or such like, handle them not to take the best; yet if any one eat of thy dish, take no heed what he doth.

29. Put not a bit in thy mouth, untill the former be swallow'd; let them be such that puff not up thy cheeks notably. Serve not thy self with both thy hands, to carry a morsel to thy mouth, but make use of the customary way, that is the left.

30. Fill not thy glass in such a manner, that the wine run over, and fall upon the Table-cloth.

31. Drink not with meat in thy mouth; call not for drink then, speak not then; fill not thy glass to drink, and drink not while thy next companion drinketh, or he who sitteth at the upper end of the table.

32. When

32. When thou drinkest gaze not here and there.

33. Drink not too leisurely, nor too hastily, or as chawing the Wine, nor too often. Before and after that thou hast drunk wipe thy ⟨lip⟩s and breath not with too great a noise then, or ever, for it is an uncivil thing.

34. Clense not thy teeth with a table-cloath ⟨or⟩ napkin, or with thy finger, fork or knife; ⟨m⟩uch worse would it be to do so with thy ⟨na⟩iles, but use thy pick-tooth: It seemeth like⟨w⟩ise uncomely to clean them at the table, ⟨w⟩ere it so that the others do not the same, and ⟨th⟩at it were the custom of the best bred.

35. Rince not thy mouth with wine, to spit it ⟨o⟩ut before others, but when thou shalt be risen ⟨fr⟩om the table, usually wash thy hands with ⟨th⟩e others. For the mouth it seemeth unfit to ⟨w⟩ash it in mens presence; and therefore when ⟨w⟩ater is given at the table, one ought to wash ⟨o⟩nly ones hands.

36. It is a thing little praise-worthy, and ⟨n⟩ow a days almost out of use, to call upon the ⟨c⟩ompany to eat; principally too often, and ⟨w⟩ith importunity, for it seemeth, that one be⟨r⟩eaveth them of their liberty; much lesse ⟨s⟩houldest thou drink to others every time ⟨t⟩hou drinkest, but if one drink to thee, thou ⟨m⟩ayest refuse it civilly, rendering him thanks ⟨f⟩or his courtesie, and acknowledging that thou ⟨y⟩ieldest; or rather taste a little of the Wine,
especially

especially with men who are accustomed to it, and take a denial in ill part.

37. When others have left eating, dispatch also, and hold not thine arms upon the table, but rest thy hand only on the edge thereof.

38. It is peculiar to the chiefest of the company, to be the first to unfold his Napkin, and fall to the meat; and therefore it is the duty of others to attend patiently, without setting hand on any thing before him.

39. On the contrary part, he ought to be solicitous to begin in time to provide all, and entertain the guests, and finish all with such dexterity, that he may give time to the slowest to eat at their leasure, entertaining himself, if it be needfull, in slightfull tasting meats, or when it is lawfull to discourse at the boord, intermingling some little Relation, untill the company might make an end.

40. Be not angry at the Table whatsoever hapneth, or if so be thou be vexed, make no shew thereof, especially there being strangers at the Table; a chearfull countenance makes one dish a feast.

41. Set not thy self at the upper end, but if it be thy due, or that the master of the house would have it so, contend not much for thy going thither, that thou trouble not all the Company.

42. If one read or talk at the table, be thou attentive, and if it be expedient that thou
speak,

...peak, talk not with meat in thy mouth.

43. † Let thy Speeches be seriously reverent when thou speakest of God or his Attributes, for to jest or utter thy self lightly in matters divine, is an unhappy impiety, provoking Heaven to justice, and urging all men to suspect thy belief.

44. † In all things which are to be learned, whether it be in the contemplation of nature, or in the directions of humane actions, let no precept be neglected; for what at the first view may seem uselesse, upon the second thoughts thou mayest find worth observing.

45. Since Wisdome is the perfection of understanding, let Prudence to practise be the end of all thy Science; for thy knowledge of precepts, teaching thee what is good, is not of efficiency to entitle thee vertuous, no more than thy body in thy souls absence can expresse thee a man: therefore neglect not to adorn thy intellect with knowledg directive, nor be thou wanting in such actions as may truly crown thee happy.

46. † Content not thy self with the bare knowledge of these precepts: but when thou hast imprinted them in thy mind, expresse them in thy conversation, for Vertue consists in action, not in contemplation.

Laus Deo trino uni.

FINIS.

An Alphabetical Table.

A
Action with reverence. p.1
Action ill beseeming. ibid.
Actions preposterous. p.2
Admonitions, how to be received. p.15
Associate with men of quality, p.19
Advice how to be used. p.22
Absent to be traduced. p.37
Anger to be dissembled, when? p.15

B
Blowing the nose. p.2
Bed out of order. p.3
Back to the fire. p.4
Blaming others when to be avoided. p.22
Breaking jests, how. ibid.
Blow not upon thy meat. p.31

C
Comparison odious. p.25
Cloaths. p.17
Chamber handsome. p.3
Countenance phantastical. p.4
Conformity betwixt gesture and discourse. p.7
Contradictions to be avoided. p.26
Cap or hat, how, and when to be uncovered. p.8
Chiefest place. p.10
Congruity in ceremonies. p.12
Conversation and advice ought to be congruous. p.16

D
Drink not when thou art hot. p.4
Deportment for one being alone. p.20
Disputes how to be ordered. p.27
Deportment before inferiors. p.21
Digressions to be avoided. p.28
Deportment at the table. p.29
Drinking. p.34

E
Equals how to demean themselves. p.10
Eating in the streets. p.19
Envy and malice to be avoided. p.21
Epilogue when proper. p.25
Eat handsomly. p.30
Eyes upon other mens trenchers. p.32

F
Fare well ordered. p.5
Flatterer. p.6
Follow the fashions of thine equals. p.17
Filling a Glass. p.34

G
Gnawing the nails. p.4
Giving the right hand. p.11, 20.
Gaze

An Alphabetical Table.

Gaze not on the imperfections of others. p.23
Guests entertained. p.36

H
Hat how to be worn. p.17
Hankerchief where to be put. p.18
Hands how to be managed. p.35
Hearing of others, how. p.2
Hands both not to be used in eating. p.35

I
Inferiour how he ought to demean himself. p.9
Imperfections in nature not to be reproached. p.15
Injurious words not to be used. p.22
Justling to be avoided. p.28

K
Killing of vermine. p.5

L
Legs across. p.4
Leg not upon another. p.5
Laughing when ridiculous. p.7
Language reproachfull to be avoided. p.16
Loud speaking to be avoided. p.28
Low Speaking. ibid.

M
Misfortunes of others not to be rejoyced at. p.7
Meeting of others. p.9
Meeting superiours. p.12
Mock not things of importance. p.15
Modesty in apparel. p.17
Meat not to blow on, nor smelt at. p.31

N
Nails foul or too long. p.5
Noyse with the teeth to be avoided. p.26,33

O
Observations for walking. p.18
Opportunity in acting or Speaking to be waited for. p.24
Obstinacy in opinion to be avoided. p.27

P
Puffing the cheeks. p.6
Pity. p.7
Precedency. p.11
Passions not to be expressed by the gesture of the body. p.20
Passions to be avoided. p.21
Presenting a thing to another unseemly, when p.33
Precepts not to be neglected. p.37

Q
Qualification in Behaviour. p.10,11

R
Rubbing the teeth. p.2
Reading unseasonably. p.3
Reading in company. p.6
Rejoycing preposterous. p.13
Reprehension of others, when seasonable. p.15
Rumor not suddenly to be believed. p.16
Reviling words, how to be received with discretion. p.27

Rinsin

Rinsing and cleansing of the mouth. p.35
Reverence towards God and his actions. p.37

S

Singing or humming. p.2
Stretching out the arms. ibid.
Sneezing. ibid.
Shutting the mouth. ibid.
Spitting. p.4,5
Stooping unbeseeming. ibid.
Scorning to be avoided. p.7
Superfluous complements. p.8
Speak not sitting to thy Superior. p.9,11
Speaking to men of quality. p.12
Superiors how to be esteemed. p.12,13
Secrets not to be sought for. p.21
Saluting others. p.23
Speaking in an unknown language, improper when? ibid.
Speaking, how, and when p.25
Speaking in secret improper, when. ibid.

T

Turning the back. p.5
Teaching an equal. p.1
Titles and attributes, how be bestowed. p.1
Thou and thee when to be used. ibid.
Tediousness in all things to be avoided. p.26
Table-cloath not to be soiled. p.33

V

Visiting the sick. p.12
Untruss not in the presence of others. p.17
Undertake not beyond ability. p.26
Virtue is in action, not contemplation. p.37

W

Writing of others not to be read. p.6
Walking how. p.10
Writing of Letters. p.12
Washing hands and face. p.17
Walking with thy Superiour, how. p.20

Y

Yawning, how. p.2

The Contents.

Chap. 1. General and mixt precepts, as touching civility amongst men. p.1

Chap. 2. Of the first duties and ceremonies in conversation. p.8

Chap. 3. Of the fashion of qualifying or titling of persons to whom one speaketh, to advise them to break a jest. p.14

Chap.

New Additions
UNTO
YOUTHS BEHAVIOUR
1650. Of some LETTERS.

AS ALSO,

A Discourse upon some Innovations of Habits and Dressings; against powdring of Hair, Naked-Brests, Black Spots, and other unseemly Customes.

LONDON,

Printed for *W. Lee*, and are to be sold at the *Turks-head* in *Fleetstreet* over against *Fetter*-Lane. 1663.

New Additions 1656.

Letter from a Gentleman to a Scholar, unto whose tuition he commits his Son.

Worthy Sir:

MY long observations, and the same from many others of your vertuous deport[m]ent in the world, and especially of that [so]und integrity, found in you, in that pro[fes]sion which you spend your time, hath easi[ly] overcome my reason, and confirmed my [ju]dgement, that you are the fittest of all o[th]er, to whom I, as an indulgent Father, com[m]it the tuition of this my little Sonne, of [wh]ose instructions in the wayes of vertue, [no]w in his tender years, I am, as nature binds [me], no lesse provident of, than of his vyands, [sin]ce I do certainly know, that without the [on]e the other will but foster a lump of rude[nes]se, producing nothing but the sad effects of [ou]r original depravation. Education there[for]e the Nurse of Youth, and life and honour [of] after-years, I do hereby on his behalf ear[nes]tly sollicite, from you, whom I have oft ob[ser]ved to give life to your precepts by your [ow]n good example; to particularize in any

thing

thing which tends to the Education of Youth, an enemy to your daily and prosperous performances; yet that love I bear to my Son, and my earnest care for the bettering of his better part, will plead my excuse, if I shall only tell you, that to have his first age watered with the wholesome and sound doctrine of fearing God, and reverencing his Superiours, will felicitate his life here, and very much comfort him in the expectation of that hereafter; To which end, I would have his tender soul daily pressed with the solid and constant pinciples of Christianity, which being well ingraffed, will serve as a Shield against all destructive temptations, and by Gods assistance make him a Conqueror, over all those solicitous affections which proceed from nature depraved. In the Moral Vertues, I do desire he may be instructed, in that his thoughts may be vertuously inclined to act what's congruous to right reason in every relation which it shall please God to fix him in : All which, the towardlinesse of his nature, I hope will facilitate, especially meeting with that aptnesse of Doctrine, which your industry doth daily infuse; to which I seriously desire a blessing from God, and so rest,

Your very Loving Friend,

A. B.

His

His Answer.

Sir:

Received yours, together with your little Son, and do very much blesse God that I [ha]d so pregnant and ample care for his good [ed]ucation, heartily wishing it may be a present to many others, who seem so far from [de]siring it, that they think neither God nor [n]ature doth tye them to further regard of [th]eir Children, than to afford them food and [r]aiment: but how far that care falls short of [th]at is required from Parents, I appeal to the [sa]d effects thereof, prophanenesse towards [G]od and his Religion, and the daily breach of [al]l Laws of civil society; to abstruct all which [as] far as in me lies, I have alwayes thought [m]y duty, and such a charge, that if I should [fai]l in the performance, I cannot with any reli[gi]ous or reasonable thought expect other than [a] heavy plague from that divine hand, which [in] Justice cannot suffer so great an offence to [b]e unpunished. Let others of my profession [th]ink as legally of their charge as they please, [im]agining that their gain ought chiefly to be [co]nsidered, and their own case preferred before [th]at efficacious sedulity and vigilancy which [is] required; yet their lazy example shall (I [tru]st in God) never sway me otherwise, than [w]ith all care possible to avoid it. And truly I [co]nceive my conscience will remain the clear[er], and much labour in Repentance for so

great

great and fearfull omission will be saved, the content which my soul doth receive from the contemplation of my performances in the duty of my profession, is, if nothing else should be offered, sufficient satisfaction. Your desire Sir, of your Sons early teaching to fear God, I shall with all possible diligence promote, and with my utmost endeavours, season his youth with the Precepts of Vertues Moral, to the end his life may be happily comfortable to himself, and opportunely prove good example for others to move by: wherein Sir, you shall not fail to find me faithfull, who am,

Your Servant in what I may,

A. B.

A Letter from a young Scholar to his Sister, intimating his good successe in election of a Master.

Dear Sister:

MY Fathers care in placing me with such a Master, doth much rejoyce me, especially in that he is a very godly man, and doth daily instruct us how to fear God, I pray you tell my Father and Mother that I am very well used, both for my Learning and Diet; and return them many thanks for their great charge, which I know I do stand them in for my Learning and being abroad; My Master is very

carefull

carefull of us all, that we use not ill company, of some untaught boyes here in the Town, and that we come not in danger by waters. I received your last Token, for which I many times thank you, and will ere long requite it, in the mean time I rest

Your very loving Brother

S. H.

Her Answer.

Loving Brother:

I Received your Letter, and did acquaint my Father and Mother with what was contained in it, and they seemed much to rejoyce at their good hap, in placing you with such a carefull Master. I hope you do not lose time, but imploy it both to my Father's comfort and your own good. Learning will be no burthen, and if all things else fail you, it may serve instead of them, and maintain you like a man; Therefore I hope you will mind your Master to follow his directions. My Father doth very much desire that you may profit and proceed in Learning, for he doth intend you shall go to the University: my Uncle doth much admire he hath not heard from you, and therefore a Letter to him would be very welcome. My Cozens remember them to you, and desire to hear from you: So I rest

Your loving Sister

H. H.

The Copy of a Letter to a Friend, touching his Powdered Head of Hair.

Sweet Cozen:

SInce thy late coming from the University to an Innes of Court, I have observ'd thou hast very suddenly leapt out of the modest garb of the Colledge, into the far side of the Mode of the Ladies Servants of the *New Exchange*. Truly for a handsome, neat, fashionable suit of cloathes, agreeable to thy rank, I shall rather commend than blame thee. Something there is allowable that way, especially for a young man *vivere more loci,* so as an eye be had to that deceitfull piece, called the Heart, that it flye not out too farre in point of affectation. But one thing I did observe, when I first met thee, at my last being in *London*, that I must needs tell thee a piece of my mind in, as a Friend, in a few sudden Lines : That witty Noddle of thine, was put into such a pure modified Trim, the Dislocations of every hair so exactly set, the whole Bush so curiously Candied, and thy Natural Jet, so exalted into a perfect Argent, that I had much ado to own thine honest Face. Sweet Cozen, thou art even become a very bonny fellow methinks; but if I had met thee on a sudden in this dresse, at my Rural habitation, I should have been jealous thou hadst been tampering with my Wives Maid of the Bakehouse, and the peevish Girl had bestowed a badge of her Office upon thee. Ile give thee no advice as a Divine now, for sure thou art grown Sermon proof with safety in *London.* But seriously though I have little skill in Physick, yet let me tell thee what my plain Country fancy apprehends: It is a great benefit of Nature to have the liberty of free transpiration, whereby through the curious emunctories of the Pores, she doth constantly emit and disburthen her self of superfluous Evaporations, which otherwise I am ready to think, those Sewers being stockt and choakt up with that sweet artificiall Dust, conglomerated into Dirt, by the furious acting of thy fiery Brain, may in time dissolve into distillations, and (if not obfuscate thine invention, when thou hast a disposition to court thy Mistris with some rare piece of Poesie) find a passage to thy Lungs, and Cacexicate thy pretty Corpusculum, if not in time make way for a Consumption, which I am very tender of concerning thee. And besides by the opillation of those invisible perforations, through which Nature is wont to wyer-draw spare humours into a fine spun excrescency for a supplemental handsom

Orna-

Ornament, I doubt the old stock too by vicinity, will after a while grow putrid, and fall away, and then thou wilt either look like one of my pill'd Ewes, or else must put on a beastly thing, what call you it? a Periwigge, and make thy friends put a worse interpretation upon the matter than there may be cause. Indeed, one advantage I think thou maist happily have by this Artifice, if thy Purse serve thee not to be in constant Fee with a Hackney Coachman, and thou be fain to foot it oft this Summer season, though thou shouldst maintain the stately Court-like straddle for fear of putting thy Boot-hose-tops out of the set posture, (for I hope thou wilt never have any forraign reason for it) yet thou wilt now and then put thy self into a Sweat, and then be forced to apply thy self to the learned Doctor in the chequer'd Apron, for a Recruit of a little new Dregging, and so I am confident, thy head will in a short time grow so well stockt in six-footed Cattle, that thou needest not be to seek at any time for a medicine for the Jaundies.

Sweet Cozen, I abominate sordid slovenliness, but, as a plain meaning friend, I should think it cleanly enough, and more wholsome and better exercise, to make use of a good honest course Linnen Rubber, every morning for thy Head. But I leave thee to better judgement, I must abroad into the Fields

amongst

nongst my Plough-folks and Workmen, and I am affraid thou wilt think, I might have been better busied there all this while: and truly so do I think too, but my Pen was got into a wood, ere I was aware, and could not find the way out; excuse it for once; it may be, if you think well on't, thou hast spent a few minutes as idly, as either I in writing, or thou in reading this scrible.

Sweet Cozen I am

From my House   *Thine affectionate.*
at H. *Apr.* 29.
1650.   *Cozen to serve thee.*

Discourse upon some Innovations of Habits and Dressings.

'Tis ill disclaiming against publick evils, in Popular Discourses, besides that usually they bear more of brute than fruit, and (as *Seneca* once said) serve rather for ostension of wit, than improvement of life: It may be likewise observed, that obstinate maladies never make for the honour of the Physician, and he that gives good counsel in vain, besides the loss of his labour,
in

in some sense loseth of his credit, and m[oveth] a scorn. With how little success Divi[nes] and Moralists, (the proper Physicians of [our] souls) have hitherto attended the cure of [di]seased minds, appeareth by the daily grow[th] of vice, and the numerous accession of new [e]normities.

2. Out of which great heap (amidst a[ll] these disadvantages) we have thought fit t[o] gather up one handfull; for an instance[.] Who seeth not how much sober advice, an[d] grave remonstrance hath been fruitlessl[y] spent upon the cure of that English itch o[f] running after fashions? a vanity so peculia[r] to us, that we are become the scorn of the se[-]veral Nations whence we borrow them. A[n] outlandish Painter thought he had quit him[-]self upon us with a handsome piece of Drol[-]lery, when having abstracted the habit o[f] divers Nations into one Table, and repre[-]sented a man of each Country in his Nativ[e] Apparel, he Painted an English man with a pair of Shears in his hand, as being ye[t] to seek of a fashion. I leave it to men o[f] more learning and leisure, to found out th[e] original cause of this giddy humour, whe[-]ther it be from the changeable complexio[n] of the Climate, or the peculiar influence o[f] some phantastical Planet: And truly since that *Jovius* and some others have been bol[d]

of Habits and Dressings. 55

go up into Heaven, and there arrest the [stars] with the guilt of new Heresies, and [eve]ry ordinary Astronomer accuseth them [wi]th the daily quarrels of Christendome, one [m]ight think it as lawfull to charge them with [thi]s influence also, since all of them are [bu]t humour and phansie, though (to say [tru]th) one may be much more dangerous [tha]n another. Or be it that this Island [ha]ving been called another World, and a [ty]pe, or as it were, the Contents to that [gre]at Chapter of the Universe; the ambiti[ou]s Islander pretends a right, and a claim [to a]ll customs in the world elsewhere. But [not] to waste time in calculating the Nativ[it]y of new Fashions, we may resolve it, [tha]t the mind of man, even as his body, is [lab]le to the constant invasion of new dis[eas]es. Our modern Physicians (without [que]stion) have discovered such Maladies, [as] neither *Galen* or *Hippocrates* ever knew [of]: and the humour of this age hath bro[ken] out with such symptomes of phantasti[ci]ty, as elder times would have blushed [at:] but in the vicissitude of Vanity, you shall [obse]rve this method, that though each take [its] own turn in its own time, yet never any [old] custome went out, but to give way to a [wor]se. Pride cannot be proud enough, till [it b]e grown prodigious. With what a stu[pe]nd[o]us care our young Monsieur *Ala mode*
hath

hath stretched and tired every Mechani[c] to become a tripartite Monster; look u[pon] his powdred head, you will think him [a] Meal-man, by his Codpiece a Satyr, or [some] wild type of his Ancestor *Adam*, late thrust out of Paradise, and by his feet a Gy[ant], whom no shooe can fit, but such as [are] made upon the Last of *Hercules*: Certainly i[n] this design he hath out-thriven his own ho[pe] and is become the subject of a double wonde[r] and is equally though differently ballance[d] both in the admiration of fools, and scorn [of] wise men.

3. But we shall not land our discourse o[n] this shore, but as coasting by with this sho[rt] reflection, pass on in our *Amazonian* Voy[-] age, upon a discovery of some late exorbi[-] tances in the other Sex. It must not be den[i-] ed, but that the indulgence of Nature hat[h] left a greater liberty to women, than unt[o] men in point of curiosity in Apparel. [A] priviledge which men ought not to env[y] them, because what ever imbellishment[s] Woman bestows on her own beauty, is to b[e] adjudged but her duty, and an effect of th[e] subordinate complacency which she owe[s] to the Male, whose servant she is, by creatio[n] And yet Nature hath limited this priviledg[e] of women with strict Laws, and those n[ot] to be transgressed without an high offen[ce] again[st]

...inst it self; and to offend Nature is one ...the highest offences; for to offend her, is ...offend her highest Author, that is, God ...self. Now the dictate of this natural ...w is, that no woman use any habit or ...m of Attire, but such as contributeth to ... truest beauty, and the beauty of that ...uty is their modesty; for since original ... subjected them to the necessity of Appa-...they must ever remember to wear it as ...Ornament of Decency, not of Vanity: ...: if by this rule one should examine that ...tart impudence of naked Breasts, with ...t other apish trick of Patch'd Faces, it ...uld put men of sober thoughts to great ...azement, when they shall find a new-born ...v of Custome to have defaced the reve-...d old Law of Nature; I would ask whe-...r these baring of the breasts and shoulders, ...the loop-holes for chastity to look out at, ...ather are they not the sally-ports of *Ve-*...? and the amorous darting places, from ...ence *Cupid* at advantage discharges his ...illery? Certainly one may believe that ...us in her life time (before she put on such ...bes of Immortality, as succeeding Poets ...e since cloathed her with,) would scarce ...e admitted *Mars* in publick to so open ...interview. I know their excuse is at ...d, 'tis the Fashion, and Fashion is a Cu-...ne, and Custome is a Law, or a Nature, or both. But admit it a Custome, and a Fashion, yet it is so far from civil, that the civil Heathens would from all Ages downward hav abhorred it, even to jealousie: the Persian and Turkish women hardly daring to let the Sun peep upon their faces: and to those our Ladies, whom Custome hath inured to such a posture and degree of Nakedness, to think it no apparition of dishonour, to say the least, if it be not an affront to virtue, I dare say, 'tis a strange dissembling of it; and at the least it is an Innovation, and a meer piece of refined Barbarism, as if it were done in a design to facilitate an accommodation with those American Ladies in the Court of King *Atabalipa* or *Pocahuncas*; and having once landed there, it may hazard them upon a shrewd prospect of heresie, and by degrees, and insensible insinuations, hint them upon the dangerous approaches of brutish Adamitism: so natural it is for Error to beget Error, and transmit it self from bad to worse, and of Phantastical, to become dogmatical: as we see Evils ripen with time, in time Scabs grow Botches, and Snakes become Serpents.

4. Now for that other new trick of pouncing the face with an atorne imagery of Patches: It hath so much of Monster and prodigy in it, that it is a hard matter to resolve it into its original principles, or describe it

in its firſt riſe: Whether it be, that in theſe warlike times, *Venus* in a frolick of kindneſs, or an amorous ſympathy with thoſe late Maſculine ſufferers, is pleaſed to put on her ſervant *Mars* his skars: or rather did it ariſe from our neighbour Kingdome of *France?* and if from thence (though *France* be fantaſtical enough) yet in this we may excuſe that Nation, as having taken up the Faſhion rather for neceſſity than novelty, inaſmuch as thoſe French pimples have need of a French Plaiſter. And we know that houſes and apparel were firſt made for need, and after for ornament, and who can tax their witty Pride, which could ſo cunningly turn Botches into Beauty, and make Uglineſs Handſome. Others, perhaps, will drive it farther off, and father it upon the Indies, and ſo make it another piece of refined Barbariſm. The Copy whereof (taken from that Pagan uſage of Printing the Volume of their bodies all over with Apes and Monkies) our Ladies here have abſtracted to a finer Character, and abridged it into the Title Page of the Face: Herein being much befriended by the ingenious Artizan, whoſe skilfull hand (far exceeding him that firſt contracted the Decalogue and *Pater noſter* within compaſs of a Penny) is able to vie wonder it ſelf: He will paſs you a Camel through the eye of a Spaniſh Needle, without a Miracle, and rarifie a Coach and Horses into the dimension of two Fleas; by this means the *Exchange*, (that arsenal of choice vanities) is furnished with a daily supply, and variety of beauty-spots; cut out in diminutive Moons, and Suns, and Stars, Castles, Trees, Towns, Birds, Beasts, Fish, and all other living creatures, wherewith beauty is turned into a Landskip, and ambitious pride hath in a manner abstracted *Noah*'s Ark, yea the Creation it self into a Ladies Cheek, that the concurrence of so many rare perfections, one might say there wanted nothing, except it be that, which *Tacitus* said, was wanting to the accomplishments of *Nero*'s Mistress *Poppaa Sabina* : *Cui erant omnia præter bonam mentem.* But from what Countries, or for what causes soever women have assumed this wild custom of Spotting their Faces, and baring their Skins, though I dare not in the down-right words of that learned King *James* affirm, *That whoever used it, either was or would be*——Yet in the language of another mighty Emperour, even *Julius Cæsar* himself, I shall not fear to pronounce, *That a chaste woman ought to avoid, not onely fault, but the suspition too* : and why should a *Lucrece* or a *Penelope* appear in the Dress of a *Cleopatra* or a *Messalina* : and we know who hath bidden us abstain from appearance of evil. But if no personal resentment *of Habits and Dressings.*

[…]ntment of honour can perswade them to [se]lf-reforming; in the next place (with sub[m]ission) I should think it worth the care of [th]ose in Power, to mortifie such an upstart [hu]mour by a Law. In all ages, and all pla[ce]s it hath been the wisdom of States to sup[pr]ess Innovations, whereof the Turks and [Pe]rsians are to this day exceedingly jealous; [an]d therefore will indure no change of man[ne]rs or habits; and *Plato* of old was so [str]ict, that he would not admit so much as a [ne]w Tune, or a Jig to be Sung in his Com[m]on-wealth, lest it should stir up new hu[mo]urs in the people, to the disturbance of the [La]ws, and unsettling the Government: But [ab]solutely forbids young people to change [the]ir fashions at pleasure. And no less com[m]endable was the care of the old *Romans*, [in] appointing their *Censores morum*, whose [of]fice it was to punish and restrain all ex[amp]les and exorbitancies in Fashions, Habits, [an]d Behaviours. The disusage whereof, [per]haps is no small encouragement to the [lu]xury and looseness of these times. And [ho]w well it were to revive such a Magistrate [in] good earnest, we may remember how [goo]d use the late Lord-Chief Justice C[oke] [ma]de of it, though but in a jest: In a time [wh]en most of our English Gallantry of both [Sex]es, was so far infected with the Jaundies [of y]ellow starch'd Bands and Cuffs, he found

E 3 out

out a queint invention, to execute that odious Innovation at the Gallows, by commanding the common Hangman to do his office in that Equipage. And for these later phantasticalities (sith the weakness of this Discourse cannot hope to make them) we shall so far cooperate with his Lordships Note, as to bequeath them to the same Fate: it being but just, that what began with Vanity should end with Infamy.

FINIS.

Added

Added in the Year 1663.

The first entrance of a Youth in the University.

HE that will make good proficiency in his travel of study at the University, [must] first be well furnished with Languages, [seeing] that is a place for the learning of things, [not] words: for though many come Peda[nt]ues from the University, none should be [made] there. But if by thine own idleness, or [slug]gish Genius, or by the hasty indulgence [of] thy overweaning Relations to speed thee [on] the lash; thou shouldst be admitted [to] this place with a too raw and ill prepared [sto]mack, for the digesting that solider part [of] learning thou there must be fed with: [be] sure then to keep close to the Directi[on] of thy Tutor, and let thy prudence sup[ply] thy want in Learning; keeping thy [tong]ue with a strict Raine, which other[wise] will soon be the instrument of thy ut-

E 4 ter

ter ruine; running thee into such absurdities, as their guilt (not to be wiped off by an after-care and study) will make thee a confident *Rachel*, or a modest foole.

2. Being thus fitted for a Tutor, who (from the prudent choice of those that have the disposing of the young Student) is presumed to be discreet and able, it were to forestall the Market, or rather to take the work out of an Artists hands, to lay down a series of particular Precepts, for his Instructions and Government.

But because the Pupill is not always in the Tutors eye, and the first miscarriages or good deportment, do usually prejudice his esteem, or make fair way for his future reputation with the Society, to whose view and inquiry he is chiefly at first exposed; it will not be amiss to take notice of some of these following Cautions and Admonition.

Choose for thy constant associate or Chamber-fellow, one that is famed for Schollarship and Sobriety, (as quickly thou shalt learn who they are:) so shalt thou have a Pilot to steere thee between the two Rocks of Duncery and Rabellisme, which most Freshmen (for with that name thou must be contented,) are in danger to fall upon, finding themselves freed from the Pedagogical bondage, and Masters of the greatest part of their time, are desirous to indulge a little in the novel Recreations

tions of the place, till unawares, and even insensibly they are habituated in debauchery.

Make no greater boasts of the School from whence you come, than thy own proficiency will be able to attest, least thine own mouth convict thee for a Loyterer amongst good Schollars: it being an harder matter to rub off the disgrace of the one, than gain the repute of the other.

Let there be no day without the addition of a line, to the Portraicture of a learned man: for however thou mayst conceit thou hast outstript thy companions, by the advantages of thy School or parts, to rest for a while: in time, the continually slow-moving Snaile, will get before the presumptuous loytering Hare.

Let thy first performance in publick exercise be done with the utmost of thy skill and indeavours, with the inspection and advice of thy faithfull friend or companion, that is of greater standing than thy self: For what may seem well done to thy self, or another lately removed from the *Ferula*, will perhaps disrellish an Academical pallate.

Discourse not even a truth, much less impertinent mistakes, without too great an heat carried out with impudent conceited gestures, badges of empty braines, or childish tempers, nor yet with too much modesty, which
though

though it be the symptome of an ingenuous spirit; yet alwayes takes off from your present province, and gives ground to others to trample on your easier nature.

Speak no reproachfull words of any, especially thy superiours, or those by whom thou maist hope to gain preferment: for injuries received are often written on Marble Pillars, and set up as a *ne plus ultra* to a mans preferment, when all the water wherewith thy good words and actions have been written, cannot obliterate such black Characters.

Follow not thine own juvenile fancy, in the course of thy study, but use a method by the advice of some prudent director; which may be subservient and usefull to that course of living thou intendest for the future.

Buy not nor borrow any Book but for thy present use; for a new Book sharpens the appetite of the Student, if he no sooner possess him, than he studies him: but read no Pamphlets for their novel or pleasing titles, but rather a few substantial Authors, which well digested (as a fountain) will affoard more clear and wholsome learning, than all those new-found rivulets which issued only from them.

Own no opinions either in Divinity or Philosophy, till time shall ripen thine understanding, least a frequent changing of thy mind argue an unconstant levity or want of
judgment:

judgment: but in the mean while, compose thy self according to the example of the best livers, in matter of practice; taking deep root in fundamentals: and so having taken a strict survey of all, thou shalt have time enough to manifest, that thy perswasions are founded on reason, not fancy.

Be not slily sneaking, nor insolent in thy carriage, but affable to all, especially those who may envy thy proficiency: for envy hath ruined deserts; and a blot is sooner fastened upon a mans good name, than clearly wiped off.

If it be possible, gain a true friend, whose prudent advice will supply the defect of farther instructions: and having made use of these, thou maist furnish thy self out of thine own stock for the future, and likewise be helpfull to others.

Additions

Additions to Youths Behaviour.

† DO not think that thou canst be a friend to the King, whilst thou art an enemy to God: if thy crying iniquity should invite Gods judgements to the Court, it would cost thy Soveraigne dear, to give them entertainment.

† Let thy recreations be manfull, not sinfull; there is a great vanity in the baiting of Beasts: the Bears and Bulls lived quietly enough before the fall; it was our sin that set them together by the ears; rejoyce not therefore to see them fight, for that would be to glory in thy shame.

† Honour and obey thy natural Parents, although they be poor; for if thy earthly Parents cannot give thee riches and honour, yet thy heavenly Father hath promised thee length of dayes.

† Labour to keep alive in thy breast, that little sparke of cælestial fire, called conscience; for conscience to an evill man is a never dying worm, but unto a good man, it's a perpetual feast.

† If thou wouldst enjoy true content, live peaceably in that vocation unto which providence hath called thee; meddle not with another

another mans trade and employment, but learn to move in thy own sphear, and to mind thine own particular function.

† If thou art yet unmarried, but intendest it, get thee a wife modest, rather than bautifull; meddle not with those Ladies of the Game, who make Pageants of their Cheeks, and Shops of their Shoulders, and (contrary to all other Trades,) keep open their Windowes on the Sabbath-Day, impudently exposing their nakedness to the view of a whole Congregation, which *Eve* modestly covered, when there was no man in the world present save only her Husband; black Patches are an abomination in the sight of the Lord; and that when God and Satan shall divide their flock, (it will be as with *Laban* and *Jacob*) the spotted and ring-streaked will fall to the Devils share. Joyn not therefore thy self unto an Harlot, unless thou hast a mind to hire a guide to lead thee to Hell.

An Alphabetical Table, explaining the Words and Terms of all Sciences, Arts and Learning, most frequently used in the several Titles and Names of Books, according to their Subjects they treat of; with the examples of many men, famous in the following Sciences.

A

Abridgments, shortning of any writing, by contracting together the marrow and best of it, whether in Divinity, History, Law, or any other Science, of which many are extant.

Adages, Proverbs or common sayings, in what language soever; as *Erasmus* for the Latine, *Cotgrave* for the French, *Howell* for the English.

Alchimy, the Art of distilling or drawing quintessence out of Mettals by fire, seperating the pure from the impure, setting at liberty such bodies as are bound and imprisoned, and bringing to perfection, such as are unripe; of which *Paracelsus*, Dr. *French*, with many others, have most learnedly written.

Alimony, a yearly allowance from the Husband to the Wife, being parted; of which you may read sufficiently in *The Womans Lawyer*.

Anagram, an invention by altering the places of the Letters of ones name, to make another word or sentence.

Analogies, proportions, or resemblances of things.

Analysis, such as resolve, or unfold an intricate matter, or distributing the whole into parts, few Sciences but some are made upon it.

Anatomy, the incision or cutting up the body of man or beast as Chyrurgeons do, to discover the substance, actions, and use of every part; Dr. *Read*, Dr. *Harvey*; likewise *Crooke* and *Parry* have largely written

ten upon that Subject.

Annotations, Paraphrases, Commentaries, or Expositions, on any Science; as the Assemblies, Dutch, *Diodati*, *Mayer*, *Trap*, with others upon the Bible; few Sciences without some Expositors.

Anonymus, a book without the Authors name, as, *The whole duty of man*, *Doctor and Student*, with many more, *Ignotis authoribus*.

Anthologie, treating of Herbs and Flowers, *Gerrard* and *Parkinson*, to whom, none are to be compared

Antiquities, treating of things past, famous were Sr. *Henry Spelman*, Mr. *Selden*, *Elias Ashmole* Esq; *Rich. Verstegan* and now Mr. *Dugdale* living.

Apology, a defence or excuse of any thing, as Sr. *Rich. Baker's* Apology for lay mens writing in Divinity.

Apophthegms, brief and pithy speeches or sentences, of any renowned personages; as *Lycosthenes*, Sr. *Francis Bacon*, do elegantly shew.

Architecture, the art of devising, framing or drawing Plots in Building; famous in this Art were *Van Vincent Scamozi*, *Ignoli Jones*, and Mr. *Edw. Carter*.

Arithmetick, the art of numbring, in which famous was *Record*, *Wingate*, *Johnson*, *Moore*, and now Mr. *Smart* living in the Poultry.

Astrology, a Science which tells the reasons of the Stars and Planets motions, and foretels things to come.

Astronomy, a Science (not much different from the former,) that teacheth the knowledge of the course of the Planets, Stars, and other cœlestial motions, in which Sciences Mr. *Lilly*, Mr. *Booker*, Capt. *Wharton*, Mr. *Wing* and others, have attained to a very great knowledg.

B

Baptisme, a washing or dipping in water, a baptizing of children, an Ordinance commanded by God, and defended by the witest of men.

Botannicke, belonging to Herbs, Mr. *Morgan* and Mr. *Coles* being excellent Herbalists.

Brachigraphy,

Brachigraphy, a short hand of writing, as a letter for a word.

C

Casuist, one that writes or is well seen in Cases of Conscience; as those two famous Divines and Casuists, Dr. *Sanderson* and Dr. *Taylor*, the one Bishop of *Lincoln*, and the other Bishop of *Downe* and *Conner* in *Ireland*.

Catalogue, a roule of names, or Register, a Cataloging of Books, which Mr. *London* Bookseller of *Newcastle*, hath published.

Characters, marks, signes, seals, or prints upon any things: a branding Iron.

Chymistry, the art of dissolving mettals, and of extracting the quintessence out of any thing. Dr. *Currer* an approved author in the art of Chymistry.

Chyromancy, or Palmestry, a kind of divination practised by looking on the lines or marks of the hands; an art still in use among fortune-tellers, *Ægyptians* and Juglers.

Chyrurgery, we commonly pronounce it Surgery, it signifieth originally the work of the hand, but it is commonly taken for the art of curing or healing of wounds and sores; Mr. *Woodall*, Mr. *Edw.* and Mr. *Will. Molins*, famous in the art of Chirurgery.

Chorography, the exact description of some Kingdome, Countrey, or particular Province of the same: Mr. *Cambden*, and Mr. *Speed* most famous Chorographists.

Chronology, a speaking of times, or the art of numbering the years from the beginning of the world; endeavoured by Mr. *Isaackson*, *Dionysius Petavius*, and Mr. *Will. Howell*.

Classical, most approved Authors, whether Divine or Humane, such as tend to edification; as the Works both Moral and Historical, of grave and learned *Plutarch*, &c.

Comedies, Plays or Interludes, kind of Fables; *Terence*, *Plautus*, *Shakspeare*, *Ben. Johnson*, *Beamont* and *Fletcher*, excellent Comedians.

Commentaries, many on the Bible, *vide* **Annotations**.

Compendium, an abbreviation of a Book or Science;

...ence; as *Wollebius* his *Compendium of Divinity.*

Concordances, ordinary for places of Scripture, agreeing one with another, often explaining one another; as the laborious Work of Mr. *Cotton*, enlarged by Mr. *Newman*; and a more brief Concordance of Mr. *John Downham.*

Cookery, a curious dressing of flesh, fish, or foul for the Table; the accomplished artists were Mr. *Murrell*, Mr. *May*, with divers others.

Cosmography, a description of the world; which Sr. *Walter Rawleigh*, and Doctor *Heylin* have most largely described.

Curiosities, rare inventions of several Arts; described by famous *Gaffarel*, in his *Unheard of Curiosities.*

D

Dialling, of, or pertaining to the making and ordering of Dials, many being famous in this so rare an Art.

Dialogues, the discoursing of two men, or more, in writing or in words; as *Erasmus*, and *Corderius Colloquies.*

Dictionary, in Greek is called a *Lexicon*, a Book wherein hard words and names are mentioned and unfolded; as *Riders*, *Thomas Thomasius*, *Wase*, and the Poetical Dictionary.

Distillation, a dropping down, or distilling in a Limbeck; vide Alchimy.

Divination, a presaging or foretelling of things to come, belonging to Astronomers.

Divinity, pertaining to the knowledge of the Godhead, upon which the Fathers of the Church have many volumes; as also Bp *Andrews*, Bp *Hall*, Bp *Usher*, Mr *Leigh*, and other learned authors have largely written upon Divinity.

Dogmatical, of, or pertaining to a sect or opinion.

Drollery, a facetious way of speaking or writing, full of knavish wit.

Duel, a fight between two, with their seconds standing by, prohibited by Proclamation, and discountenanced by *Voetius*, Sr. *Francis Bacon*, and divers other learned Writers.

E

Elegies, mournfull Verses, or Funeral Songs, upon deceased

deceased persons to be lamented; as *Oxford* and *Cambridge*: besides divers other Poets, upon the death of Prince *Henry* Duke of *Glocester*, and *Henrietta Maria* Princess of *Orange*.

Elements, are the most simple bodies extant in nature, from the several participations of whose qualities, all mixed bodies have their several beings, and different constitutions: they are four in number, Fire, Air, Water and Earth. Element in the singular number stands for one of those; sometimes it signifieth a letter, as A, B, C, sometimes the first foundation or principal of a thing.

Emblems, moral sentences, by way of devices or pictures: as *Quarls*, *Withers* and *Farloe*, do shew in their **Emblems**

Enthusiasm, an inspiration, a ravishment of the spirit, divine motion, poetical fury; explained by Mr. *Cansabone*.

Ephemerides, Bookes wherein daily acts are Registred, a Journal or Diary; commonly taken for a Book of Astronomy, (in use among such as erect figures to cast mens Nativities,) by which is shown, how all the Planets are placed, every day and hour of the year; as *Wing* hath shewed in his **Ephemerides**.

Epigrams, short Poems upon several kinds of Subjects; as *Owens* and Sr *Tho. Moores* for example.

Episcopacy, of, or belonging to a Bishop; for the defence of which, read Dr. *Hammon* and other learned Writers.

Epitaphs, inscriptions or writings, set upon a Tomb, most commonly in praise, or lamentation of the party there buried; of which many are in *Stowes* Survey of *London*.

Epitomies, *vide* **Abridgements**.

Essays, trials or endeavours; Sr. *Walter Rawleigh*, Sr. *Francis Bacon*, and *Rich. Braithwait* Esq; having written upon them.

Etymology, the true exposition or derivation of a word; which Mr. *Blunt*,

The first Table.

Blunt, and Mr. *Philips* shew in their *English Dictionary*.

Ethicks, Books belonging to Moral Philosophy.

Examples, precedents, patterns, or Coppies to follow, of which many are extant; as of Mr. *Getting*, Mr. *Hodder*, Mr. *Cocker*, Mr. *Billingsly*, and Mr. *Davies*, with others.

Expositions, see **Annotations**.

Eucharist, the Communion, or Sacrament of the Lords Supper; excellently treated upon by Mr. *Dyke* and Mr. *Dod*, with divers others.

F

Fables, wherein beasts and trees, &c. are feigned to speak; *Æsop* excelling all others in writing of **fables**.

Faulconry, Hawk-managing, or the art of keeping hawks; famous were Mr. *Birt*, M. *Turbervile*, and Mr. *Latham*.

Fencing, the art of using and handling Weapons, usefull and necessary for all Gentlemen.

Fire-works, shows or pastimes made upon the land or water by fire; treated of by Dr. *Bates*.

Fishing, the art of Angling, or catching and ordering of fish; discoursed upon by Mr. *Isaac Walton*, and Mr. *Taverner*.

Folio, the full breadth of the Paper, being but two leaves in the sheet.

Fortification, making strong a Town, to keep out the enemy; in which Mr. *Faulconberg* was very ingenious.

Fowling, the art of taking Birds, either by land or by water; explained by *Gervase Markham* Esquire.

Frontispiece, a Title graven in brass, set at the beginning of a Book.

G

Gaging, the measuring of Vessels for Wine or Beer.

Gardening, the art of keeping and dressing of fruit and flowers; *The French Gardener* in 12°, a most excellent piece.

Genealogy, a description of ones lineage, stock or pedigree, as that which is most commonly bound before Bibles.

Geography, a description of the earth, by its parts and its limits, scituations, Inhabitants, Cities, Rivers,

The first Table.

Rivers, fertility, and other observable matters; vide **Chorography** and **Cosmography**.

Geometry, an art of due proportion, consisting in lineaments, forms, distances, and greatness; famous in this art were *Euclid* and Dr. *Wybard*.

Grammer, a Book containing the first beginning of any Language; as *Lily* for the Latin, *Gambden* for the Greek, chiefly to be learned of all scholars.

Graving, belonging to the art of **Calcography**, or cutting effigies, or fancies in Copper; in which art famous was *Callot*, *Marshall* and *Paine* deceased; and now Mr. *Faithorn*, Mr. *Lombart*, Mr. *Hertochs* and Mr. *Loggain* living.

H

Hawking, vide **Faulconry**.

Heraldry, an office, to proclaim Peace or War; also to examine Gentlemens Arms: *Tho. Rawling* Esq; also Mr. *Knight*, and Mr. *Nower*, with Mr. *Carter*, Mr. *Guillim*, and Mr. *Peckham*, famous in **Heraldry**; also Mr. *Gambden*, and now Mr. *Dugdale* King at Arms.

Herbary, *Gerard* and *Parkinson*, most famous in describing all kinde of **Herbs**; vide **Bottannicks**.

Heresies, (as the Fathers describe it,) misbeliefs in some points of faith, contrary to the doctrine universally received in the Church of *England*; Mr. *Paget*, and Mr. *Ross*, having described at large the errors of most Hereticks.

Heteroclites, taken for a noun, that hath a different way of declining; explained by Mr. *Robinson* in *Lillies* Grammer.

Hieroglyphicks, misterious Characters, or Pictures used among the *Ægyptians*: they expressed holy Scriptures; treated of by *Henry Estienne*, Lord of *Fossez*, in French, and translated into English by *Tho. Blunt* Gent.

History, writing of actions of War or Peace, of the Government of any Countrey, or of the whole world; famous Historians were *Matthew Paris*, Dr. *Fuller*, and Sr. *Walter Rawleigh*.

Homolies, Speeches, or Sermons, appointed to be

be read in Churches.

Horology, belonging to the art of **Dialling**, or making of Clocks; Mr. *Foster* and others being artificial in it.

Horsmanship, the skill of riding, managing, or breeding of Horses; *Degray, Markham*, and Mr. *Green* being skilfull therein.

Husbandry, tillage, dressing or trimming of land, by graffing, plowing, or setting; Mr. *Austen*, and Mr. *Blith*, having treated of this art.

Hunting, a sport used in catching of hares and dear; treated of by Mr. *Gardener* and others.

Hymns, spiritual Songs or *Psalms*, sung to the praise of God, as *Davids Psalms*; collected into English Meeter, by *Thomas Sternhold, John Hopkins* and others.

I

Jests, conceits and inventions for making of mirth; as the reading of *Skogain*, and *Arches* jests.

Jewelling, the art of cutting and setting of Jewels; in which Mr. *Gyffard* was very ingenious; besides many others being very dexterious.

Index, a Table of a Book, a summary, a mark, sign or token; as Mr. *Ash* of Grays-Inn, who wholly employed his study in making Tables to the Law.

Itinerary, a Commentary on things fallen out in journeys; it is used adjectively, as appertaining to a journey; as Mr. *Burton*'s Commentary on *Antoninus Itinerary*.

Institutes, Laws made by Parliaments, or Orders appointed by particular men, for the obtaining such or such Sciences; famous in Institutions were *Calvin* for Divinity, *Justinian* for the Civil Law, and Sr. *Edward Cooke* for the Common Law.

L

Labyrinth, a maze, turning in and out; the two most famous were they which *Miris* King of Ægypt built, and that which *Dedalus* built for *Minos* King of *Creete*.

Law, a noble Science, by which offendors are punished, and those that are injured, righted; in which famous was *Littleton*

tleton the English Lawyer, besides many other past, and now many present.

Lecanomancy, divining by water in a bason.

Lent, a time of fourty days fasting in imitation of our Saviour; derived from the Dutch word *Lente*, which signifieth the Spring; because it happens in the Spring time; of which Dr. *Gunning* hath learnedly discoursed of late, and published in Print.

Letany, a Book of *Divine Service* used in Churches, that general Prayer for all sorts of men, in our Book of *Common Prayer*, beginning in the morning Service, *O God the Father of Heaven*, &c. the Compilers of which were Dr. *Cranmer*, Dr. *Ridley*, with other reverend Bishops.

Letters, the revealing ones mind in writing; *Monsieur de Balzac*, and *Voiture*, being exquisite Penmen in enditing.

Lexicon, an unfolding of hard words or sayings, whether Hebrew, Greek or Latine; *Scapula, Scrivelius, Crispin, Passor*, most famous for the Greek, and *Buxtorff* for the Hebrew.

Libels, printed papers, in derogation and dispraise of the State, or some particular person, to blast the reputation either of their persons, government or office.

Limning, the art of drawing, or painting the true likeness and proportion of any thing in oyle, or water colours; in which famous was *Mercus Gerardus*, Sr. *Anthony Vandyke*, with many more excellent in so rare an art.

Lyturgie, signifieth in general any publick office, but more particularly, *Divine Service*, or the function of a Minister; the *Common Prayer* of the Church now by Law established.

Logick, the art of discoursing learnedly, according to reason; famous Logicians were *Burgersdicius, Peter Ramus*, with others.

M

Magick, enchantment, or sorcery, either natural or artificial; in which famous was *John Baptista Porta*,

Porta, Mr. *Turner*, with others.

Manuscripts, things only written with the hand, not printed, but kept in writing for particular uses.

Mathematicks, arts taught by demonstration, comprehending the four liberal Sciences, viz. *Arithmetick*, *Geometry*, *Musick*, *Astronomy*, wherein the *Ægyptians* and *Caldeans* chiefly excelled; but also much delighted in, and studied by our modern Gentry, as Sr. *John Heydon*, Mr. *Moore*, Mr. *Gadbury*, Mr. *Leyborne*, with many more.

Maxims, true and general rules, either in Divinity, Law, or Physick.

Mechanick, arts, handycraft-trades, which require the labour of the hand, as tilling, cloathing, military discipline, with divers others.

Mancholly, black choler, made by adustion of the blood; also sadness, pensiveness, solitariness; fully described by Mr. *Burton*.

Merchandize, or mercature, a buying, trading, or merchandizing either by Land or Sea.

Metamorphosis, a changing of one body or figure for another; as *Ovid de Metamorph*.

Metaphysicks, a Science which treateth of supernatural things.

Midwifry, of, or belonging to the practice of the expert Widwife, treated upon by Mr. *Culpepper* and others.

Military, warlike, of, or belonging to war; Collonel *Elton*, and Collonel *Barriff*, the two chief (in English) that have written of this subject.

Monarchy, is where a Prince rules alone without a Peer, or the government of one man over many; it is that which is most agreeable to *Episcopacy*, and that which was ever accounted the best of governments, under which we now live.

Morality, civility, or good-behaviour; as *Cato* hath elegantly written of; and likewise excellent Precepts in this little Book, intituled *Youths Behaviour*.

Musick, harmony, melody, either

The first Table.

either by voice or instrument; famous Musicians were *Orlandus Lossus*, Dr. *Coleman*, Mr. *Christopher Simpson*, and Mr. *Henry Lawes*, with many others, now at present skilfull in so rare an art. It is feigned by the Poets, that *Orpheus* was so skilfull in Musick, that in playing upon his harp, the beasts of the woods, and birds of the aire, flockt near him, to partake of his sweet harmonious tunes.

Mythology, an exposition of fables; *Natalis Comes*, an elegant Mythologer.

N

Natural-history, an history of the nature of things, or things deduced from nature; *Pliny*, and the learned Sr. *Francis Bacon* having written thereof.

Navigation, sailing, or the ordering and managing of ships; Mr. *Wilsford* and others have discoursed thereon; but Sr. *Francis Drake*, *Ferdinand Magellanus*, *Oliver Vander-Nort*, Mr. *Tho. Candish* were the most famous Navigators, who sailed about the world.

Necromancy, raising up of evil spirits, or dead mens ghosts; an art not to be practised, but rather shunned; of which you may read in Dr. *Dees* actions with spirits.

Nomenclature, the numbering of names or surnames of sundry things; *Gregory* his *Nomenclature*, most usefull for all schollers.

O

Occulture, vide **Husbandry**.

Oligarchy, the state of a Common-wealth, where a few persons have all the authority; of which government we of late years have sufficiently tasted

Oratory, eloquence in writing or speaking, also a place dedicated to prayer; famous Orators were *Cicero* and *Demosthenes* with many now in our age, an art that appertains to the compleating of a Gentleman.

Orthography, the manner of true writing, there are many Books for the learing of Orthography; the *English Schoolmaster* the *Youths Book*, with divers others; which aough

//

ought not to be neglected by any, seeing it is of so great use, and general concernment.

P

Painting, vide **Limning**; Mr. *Walker*, Mr. *Hales* having discoursed thereof.

Palmestry, a divining by the palm of the hand; *ibid.* as **Chiromancy**.

Panegyricks, solemn conventions of people at some publick solemnity; also Orations made in the praise of some great persons.

Paraphrases, when things are expounded not word for word, but something added or altered by way of explanation or interpretation.

Pastorall, of, or belonging to Shepheards, sometimes made into a Play by Poets, and acted upon the stage by Players.

Perspective, the art of advantaging the sight, by the contrivance of glasses, being a branch of **Opticks**; Mr. *William Carter* artificial therein.

Philosophy, the love and study of wisdom, knowledg, and natural causes; famous in **Philosophy** were *Plato*, *Aristotle*, *Pythagoras*, *Diogenes*, *Seneca*, *Plutarch*, *Democritus* a laughing, *Heraclitus* a weeping Philosopher.

Physiognomy, an art which reacheth to know the disposition of men by their faces; Mr. *Sanders* skilfull therein.

Physick, natural phylosophy; also the art of curing by medicines; *Galen* and *Hypocrates* the two great Physicians; also famous in Physick were *Rhenodeus*, *Paracelsus*, *Barrow*, Dr. *Venner*, Dr. *Sparkes*, with many more now living.

Poetry, learned fictions in numbers or rhyme, which we call improperly rythme, or some history, or other matter in such rychme; famous in **Poetry** were *Virgil*, *Ovid*; and *Horace*, &c. with many of later times, as *Shakspear*, *Ben. Johnson*, *Beamont* and *Fletcher*; and now Sr. *John Denham*, Sr. *William Davenant*, Mr. *Shirley*, Mr. *Broome*, with divers more.

Polity, the art of war, or
safe.

The first Table.

safe government, or management of any actions, either in Church or State; which government is fully described by Mr. *Rich. Hooker*, in his unanswerable Book, called, *The Laws of Ecclesiastical Polity*.

Portraitures, pictures, images, or effigies of men cut in Copper, and commonly put before Books.

Presbytery, an eldership, a meeting of Priests, or a government of the Church, brought up by Mr. *Calvin*, which we of late have long retained, but now have left by conforming to *Episcopacy*, or government by Bishops.

Printing, an art invented by *John Guttenberge*, and being so usefull, is still much practised.

Problems, Orations or discourses ordinarily upon some moral virtues, or against their extreams; as *Aristotle*, *Antonius Zimares*, *Alexander Aphrodiseus*, do shew by way of questions and answers.

Pyromancy, divination by smoke or fire.

R

Rhetorick, the art and Science of eloquence, or of speaking well and wisely; *Butlers Rhetorick*, a great help to the learning of it.

Romances, feigned histories, either in verse or prose; *Cleopatra, Grand Cyrus, Cassandra, Astrea, Clelia,* excellent **Romances**. *Monsieur de Scudery*, a man of a sharp wit, and an elegant pen, famous in writing of them.

S

Sabbath, a celebration of the seventh day of the week, according to the Jewish Sabbath, or a day of rest; but since changed to the first day of the week, by our Saviour Christ, who is Lord of the Sabbath; Mr. *Primrose*, Mr. *Shephard*, and others, having learnedly written upon it, and proves it to be on the first day of the week, according to the resurrection of Christ.

Sermons, discourses in Divinity, explaining some Text of Scripture, or applying it; as Bp *Andrews*, Bp *Brownrigge*, Bp *Sanderson*, Dr *Taylor*, and

The first Table.

and Mr *Faringdon*, have all published in *folio*.

Short-writing, the art of writing by characters, expressed under several titles, as **Tachigraphy**, **Brachigraphy**, **Stenography**, **Zeiglography**; in which art, famous is Mr. *Shelton*, Mr. *Metcalfe*, Mr. *Rich* with others.

Similies, comparisons, when one thing is likened to another; as Mr *Spencer* hath shewed in his laborious collections of things new and old.

Solecismes, false wayes of speaking, contrary to Grammer.

Sophistry, the art of quaint beguiling, or circumvention by words or false arguments.

Staticks, a mechanick art, treating about weights and measures.

Surveying, the art of measuring of lands, woods or heaths; discoursed upon by Mr. *Leyborne*, Mr. *Eyre*, Mr. *Blagrave* and others.

Symbolography, symbole is a mark or cognizance to be known by; as the Apostles Creed is the symbale, or mark of a Christian to be known by; sometimes it is taken for a short note, or sentence, or *Motto* in arms, as *Beati pacifici*, was King *James* his Motto: and in like manner, **Symbolography** is the treating of such mottoes or cognizances.

T

Tables, the matter of any Book or Science, drawn into *Indexes* or **Tables**, as a sentence to find the substance of a whole Page; in which Mr. *Ash* of Graves Inne, bestowed much labour in reducing the Laws into **Tables**.

Theams, sentences whereupon one speaketh or writeth, commonly given as exercises to scholars.

Theology, *vide* **Divinity**.

Tithes, the tenth part of any thing, most commonly used for the tenth part of corn or hay, or other profits for the maintenance of Ministers; Sr. *Henry Spelman*, Mr *Selden*, and Mr. *Prinne*, having written in defence thereof.

Topography, is the description of some particular place or City; as Mr. *King* hath described *Chester* and the Isle of *Man*, M. *Philpot*

Philpot Kent, and Mr. *Stow* London.

Tract, a discourse, a drawing in length.

Tragedy, a play or history, beginning friendly, but ending with great slaughter; of which, Mr. *Reynolds* hath elegantly penned in thirty several Tragical Histories, called, *Gods Revenge against Murther*.

Transcripts, writings, or that which is coppied out.

Trigonometry, is the art of measuring all sorts of Angles.

Tropicks, two imagined circles in the spheres on either side, from the Equinoctial line, one of *Cancer*, the other of *Capricorn*.

Typography, belonging to Printing.

V

Vaulting, the art of leaping over horses or posts, described by Mr. *William Stokes*.

Vocabulary, consisting of words, a rendring of Latine words into English, as Mr. *Hoole* and others have done.

W

Witchcraft, enchantments, auguration, or south-saying; discovered at large by Mr. *Scot*, Mr. *Adis* and others.

Z

Zoography, a description or painting of beasts and birds; excellently described and discoursed upon by *Aldrovandus*, *Gesner*, *Johnson*, and others; and of late drawn to the life, and engraven by the ingenuous Mr. *Dunstall* and others.

Proverbia Anglo-Latina

Ordine Alphabetico.

...verbs in Latine and English, set down in ...Alphabetical Order, for the encouragement of Youth, and the better attaining to their Latine.

A

...lieno periculo fias cauti... Learn to beware by ...ther mens harms.

...onis disce bona. From ...od men learn good ...ings.

...pite ad calcem. From ...e head to the foot.

...dit in puncto, quod non ...eratur in anno. That ...ppens sometime in a ...inute, which doth not ...a year.

...amussim. To a hairs ...readth.

...candida tecta columba. ...oves flock to fair houses.

...racas Calendas. When ...vo Sundayes come together.

...ificat domum, & non habitat. He builds a house, and dwels not in it.

Amicus certus in re incertâ cernitur. A friend is best tried in adversity.

Ardua via virtutis. The way to virtue is rugged and uneasie.

Asinus asino, sus sui pulcher. The crow thinks her own birds fairest.

Asperius nihil est humili, cum surgit. Set a beggar on horseback, and hee'l ride apace.

Avarus semper eget. A covetous man is alwayes in want.

Aut Cæsar aut nullus. Either a King or a beggar.

Auri sacra fames. The hunger of gold is even to some sacred.

Aberras

The second Table.

Aberras à scopo. You are wide of the true mark.
Abundans cautela non nocet. Great caution profiteth much.
Alium silere quod voles, primus sile. Tell a secret to none.
Arator stivam tenens, hallelujah cantat. A man may serve God when he labours in his calling.
Argento respondent omnia. Money answers all things.
A verbis ad verbera. But a word and a blow.

B
Bellua multorum capitum est vulgus. The common people is a beast of many heads.
Bellum dulce est inexpertis. Warre is sweet to them that never tried it.
Beneficia in arenâ, maleficia in memoria. Good turns are soon forgot, but bad turns are always remembered.
Bilinguis non credendus est. A double tongu'd man is not to be believ'd.
Bis dat qui citò dat. He gives twice that gives when there is need.
Bona fortuna fortuita. The goods of fortune are subject to chance.
Boni balænis similes, apparent rari nantes. Good men are like whales in the ocean, which swim but here and there.
Bulla est vita humana. Mans life is but a bubble.

C
Cantabit vacuus coram latrone viator. He that has least, lives merriest.
Cedant arma togæ. Let arms give place to the gown.
Charitas incipit à seipsâ. Charity begins at home.
Cœlibem vitam agens, agit cœlestem. He that leads a single life, leads a heavenly life.
Comes facundus in viâ pro vehiculo est. A pleasant companion in the way, is as good as a Coach.
Commoditas omnis sua fert incommoda secum. Every commodity has some discommodity.
Consilium malum consultori pessimum est. Ill counsel is worst to the counsellor.
Cucullus non facit monachum. Fine cloaths are not signs of a wise man.
Cultus neglectus virum decet. A careless dress best becomes a man.
Cura facit canos. Care brings many gray hairs.

D
Dextra insidet industria fortuna, frugalitas sinistra. Indust

The second Table.

Industry is fortunes right hand, and frugality her left.

ies diem trudit. One day thrusts on another.

isce bene vivere & mori. Learn to live and dye well.

isce à sapientibus, quò fias melior: à stultis, quò cautior. Learn of wise men to be good, but of fools to be wary.

u deliberandum quod faciendum semel. A man should seriously consider what he can do but once.

lus an virtus quis in hoste requirit? In an enemy we consider not whether the conquest be by craft or valour.

optima, uxor benè morata. A good conditioned wife is the best portion.

lcius ex ipso fonte bibuntur aquæ. The sweetest water is drunk at the fountain head.

n salute frueris, caveto morbum. Keep thy self well, whilest thou art well.

E

ietas hominem exuit. Drunkenness unmans a man.

Ebrio non est fidendum. No trusting to a drunkard.

Eget verè qui sibi necessaria denegat. He may be truly said to want, who denies to himself necessaries.

Ego & Rex meus. I and my King. Cardinal *Woolsey's* proud speech.

Emit charè, qui solvit animam. He buys dear that pays his soul.

Emori per virtutem præstat quam per dedecus vivere. Better to dye nobly, than to live basely.

Errare humanum est, perseverare diabolicum. 'Tis of humane frailty to erre, but 'tis devillish to persevere in it.

Erronea conscientia necessariò peccat. An erroneus conscience necessarily sins.

Exitus acta probat, finis non pugna coronat. The end proves and crowns the work.

Exitus acta probat. The end is the tryal of every action.

Ex pede Herculem. Hercules is known by his foot.

F

Facilis descensus averni. The way to hell is easie.

Facile est (ut canem cædas) invenire baculum. It is an easie matter to find a staff

The second Table.

staff to beat a dog.
Facile est inventis addere. 'Tis easie to add to what is already invented.
Fama est præstantior auro. A good report is better than gold.
Fas est & ab hoste doceri. Instruction is good, though it come from an enemy.
Festina lente. Do things with deliberation.
Felices sanè sunt isti (quoad hanc vitam) qui nunquam aut mutuari, aut adulari coguntur. They are happy (as to the concernments of this life,) who are never driven either to borrow or flatter.
Finis belli pax. Peace is the end of War.
Fontes ipsi sitiunt. Sometimes fountains themselves are dryed up.
Fortuna opes auferre, non animum potest. Fortune may deprive me of riches, but not of my mind.
Fraus & dolus, &c. read *Patrocinari.*
Fraus & dolus nemini patrocinare debet. Fraud and deceit ought not to patronize any man.
Frangenti fidem, fides frangatur eidem. To him that breaks his trust, let trust be broken.
Fronti nulla fides. We must not judg of men by their looks.
Frustrà fit per plura, quod fieri potest per pauciora. In vain is that done by more, which may be done by fewer.
Furor arma ministrat. Fury finds arms.
Futile ne fide. Trust not a babler.

G

Galeatum serò duelli pœnitet. Bought wit is best.
Generalibus specialia derogant. A particular exception alters a general Rule.
Generosus animus vulgaria spernit. A generous mind scorns baseness.
Gladius armorum princeps. The sword is the King of weapons.
Grex totus in agris, unius porci scabie cadit. One scabed sheep infects the whole flock.

H

Habenti dabitur. Much shall have more.
Helluo librorum. An indefatigable student.
Herculis induit columnas. He undertakes a task beyond his power.
Hercules in bivio. He's at his wits end, and knows not

not whether to go. *die mibi, cras tibi.* What befalls me to day, may befall you to morrow.
Homo factus ad unguem. He's a man every inch of him.
Honi soit qui mal y pense. Ill be to him that evil thinks.
Humani generis pars una nescit quomodo vivit altera. Half the world knows not how the other half liveth.

I

Illus piscator sapit. The burnt child dreads the fire.
Ille dolet verè, qui sine teste dolet. He mourns truly, that mourns in secret.
In multiloquio non deest vanitas. In much talking, not little vanity.
In medio consistit virtus. Virtue is in the midst.
Ingenij largitor venter. Hunger breeds wit.
Ingratum si dixeris, omnia dixeris. Call a man ungratefull, and you call him the worst you can.
Inter arma silent leges. Laws are silenc'd by arms.
In vino veritas. Drunkards confess the truth.
Irritas crabrones. It is not good to wake cares asleep.
Is qui bene latuit, bene vixit. He lives well, that lives privately.
Jura inventa metu. Injust Laws were for the wicked, not for the good.

L

Laus proprio sordit in ore. It is sordid for a man to praise himself.
Linguâ amicus. A friend from the teeth outward.
Lis litem serit. Multiplying of words breeds a brawl.
Lupus in fabulâ. Here's the man we talk of.
Lupina societas. Unsociable company, where some take all the pains, and others run away with all the gains.

M

Magis illa juvant, quæ pluris emuntur. Those things which cost most, are commonly most esteemed.
Malorum elige minimum. Of two evils chuse the least.
Malè parta, malè delabuntur. Ill got, ill spent.
Malè imperatur cùm regit vulgus duces. That's an

ill government, when the common people rule their King.

Malus pater malè facit. An evil father doth ill.

Manus manum fricat. One hand washeth another.

Media tutissimus ibis. The golden mean is the best.

Moriendi mille figuræ. There is a thousand wayes to dye.

Mora trahit periculum. Delayes are dangerous.

Multi multa sciunt, sed autem nemo. Men understand many things, but few understand themselves.

Multorum manibus grande conatur opus. Many hands make light work.

Multa cadunt inter calicem, supremaque labra. Many things happen between the cup and the lip.

Mutatis temporibus, mutantur & homines. Men change with the times.

N

Ne quid nimis, Too much of one thing is good for nothing.

Necessitas aliquando cogit ad illegitima. Poverty causeth base things.

Nemo sibi nascitur. No man is born to himself.

Ne plus ultra. He is come to his farthest.

Ne sutor ultra crepidam. Let not the cobler go beyond his last.

Nescit vox missa reverti. A word once spoken is not easily recalled.

Nocet empta dolore voluptas. Pleasure bought with sorrow is a mischief.

Non est ad astra mollis è terris via. The way to heaven is very unpleasant.

Non quod non feritur, sed quod non læditur, invulnerabile est. That is invulnerable, which is not hurt, not that which is not smitten.

Non semper arcum tendit Apollo. Apollo himself is sometime idle.

Non minor est virtus quàm quærere, parta tueri. 'Tis as much pains to keep things as get them.

Non magna loquimur, sed vivimus. 'Tis better to live, than talk well.

Non pœna, sed causa, facit martyrem. 'Tis not suffering, but the cause that makes a martyr.

Nosce teipsum. Know thy self.

Nullum ad nocendum tempus angustum est malis. To wicked men, no time comes

...omes amiss to do mischief.

...nquam prospere succedunt ...es humanæ, ubi negliguntur divina. We never thrive well in the world, when we neglect our duty to God.

O

...ne nimium vertitur in vitium. Every excess is a vice; or, too much of one thing, &c.

...is homo mendax. Every man is a liar.

...e tulit punctum qui miscuit utile dulci. He hits the nail on the head, that mixeth profit with pleasure.

...ia cedunt tempori, & ...mpus æternitati. All things yield to time, and time to eternity.

...em crede diem tibi diluxisse supremum. Think every day thy last day.

...tet mendacem esse memorem. A liar had need have a good memory.

P

...pertas comes ignaviæ. Idleness causeth poverty.

...pertas non est de genere ...alorum. Poverty is no crime.

Pax quæritur bello. Peace is procured by war.

Pœna ad paucos, terro ad omnes. The punishment reaches but to a few, but the terror to all.

Plures occidit gula quam gladius. Intemperance has slain more than the sword.

Plus valet unius orando, quam mille pugnando. One man may prevaile more by prayer, than a thousand by fighting.

Probitas laudatur & alget. Virtue is commended, but we let her starve.

Proximus sum egomet mihi. Charity begins at home.

Præstat esse prometheum quam epimetheum. 'Tis better to prevent than repent.

Præstat mortuum esse, quam ignavè vivere. Better is a dead man, than a person that spends his time idly, and lives an unprofitable member of the Commonwealth.

Publica privatis, & sacra profanis præferenda. The publick is to be preferred before the private, and Religion before secular affairs.

The second Table.

Q

Qualis vita, finis ita. As thy life, so thy death.

Quicquid in buccam venerit. He speaks any thing that comes first.

Qui non vetat peccare, cùm possit, jubet. He who prohibits not sin when it lies in his power, does command sin.

Qui medicè vivit, miserè vivit. He that lives by continual physick, never wants misery.

Qui sentit onus, sentire debet & commodum. The labourer is worthy of his hire.

Qui non habet in ære, luat in corpore. He that hath no money let him be punished in body.

Qui genus jactat suum, aliena laudat. 'Tis a foolish thing to brag of ones descent or birth.

Quod fuit durum pati, meminisse dulce est. That which is grievous to suffer, is pleasant to remember.

Quod meritò pateris, patienter forre memento. Remember to bear that punishment patiently, which comes deservedly.

Quod tibi fieri non vis, alteri ne feceris. Do as you would be done by.

R

Regis ad exemplum totus componitur orbis. All follo[w] when the King leads.

Rex non habet in regno parem. The King hath n[o] equal in his Kingdom.

Rex legibus solutus est. Th[e] King is free from th[e] Laws, that is, otherwi[se] than to be directed b[y] them, not to be punishe[d] by his Subjects for tran[s]gressing them.

Ridet stultus verberatus. T[he] fool laughs when he [is] beaten.

Rigorem juris emollit equita[s]. Equity softens the rig[or] of the Law.

S

Sal sapit omnia. Salt favou[rs] all things.

Sanguis Martyrum est sem[en] Ecclesiæ. The blood [of] Martyrs is the seed of t[he] Church.

Sapientis est cernere ubi pa[r]cendi, & ubi spargen[dum]. It is a great part of wi[s]dom, to know when [to] spare, and when [to] spend.

Scelera non intrant cas[am]. Poor men live secure.

Semel in anno ridet Apol[lo]. The Gods make mer[ry] once a year.

Semel præstat quam semp[er]. Better once than [al]wayes.

Sem[

The second Table.

ber aliquid præsta, ne te navum inveniat Diabo-... Be alwayes doing somewhat, least the Devil find thee idle.

...est in fundo parsimoniæ. ...is an ill time to begin ...spare, when a man has ...more to spend.

...omnia dura Deus profuit. God hath propounded difficult things ...the wise.

...tium consensum arguit. ...lence gives consent.

...nem miseris socios habui...e dolorum. 'Tis a comfort to have companions ...misery.

...lethi consanguineus. ...eep is cousin-germane ...death.

...to episcopo, tollitur Rex. ...Bishop, no King.

...na cadunt subitó. Men ...great places fall on a ...dden.

T

...nem reddam. You shall ...ve like for like.

...ora mutantur, nos & mutamur in illis. The times ...e changed, and we are ...anged in them.

...as astræa reliquit. Justice ...fled up to heaven.

...consistit hujus vitæ felicitas; 1. *Rectâ intentione.* 2. *Corpore salutari.* 3. *Crumenâ plenâ.* Our felicity in this life consists in three things; 1. A good conscience. 2. A healthfull body. 3. A full purse.

Tutum præsidium integritas. Honesty is the best policy.

V

Ubi dolor, ibi digitus. Where the sore is, there the finger will be.

Velle suum cuique est, nec voto vivitur uno. So many men so many minds.

Veni, vidi, vici. Cæsars motto. I came, I saw, I overcame.

Veritas temporis filia. Truth is the daughter of time.

Veritas non quærit angulos. Truth seeks no corners.

Via lucis inter cruces. Afflictions bring men into the right way.

Video meliora probóque, deteriora sequor. Men commend good things, but follow bad.

Vincenti dabitur. The Conqueror carries it.

Virtus mille scuta. Virtue is instead of a thousand shields.

Virtus sola nobilitas. Virtue is the only nobility.

Vitæ est avidus, quisquis non vult mundo secum pereunte

The second Table.

unte mori. He's greedy of life, that would be willing to live, when all the world is dead.

Ultra posse non est esse. No man can go beyond his power.

Un Dieu, un Roy, un cœur. One God, one King and one heart.

Vox, & præterea nihil. Nothing but tongue.

Voluptatis commendat rarior usus. Pleasures are the sweeter, the seldomer used.

Ut in utero præparamur vita, sic in hac vitâ præparamur utero. As in the womb we are prepared for life: so in this life we are prepared for the womb, viz. the grave.

Ut redimas corpus, ferrum patieris & ignes. A man will lose all to save his life.

Vultus indicat hominem. A mans countenance betrays him.

Habet omnis hoc Voluptas,
Simulis agit fruentes;
Apiunque par volantum
Ubi grata mella fudit,
Fugit, & nimis tenaci
Ferit icta corda morsu.

Every delight hath this; that it anguisheth with pricks those that enjoy it, resembling to flying Bees, having shed his agreeable honey, flyeth away, and stingeth the hearts of them that have tasted long thereof.

An

An Alphabeticall Explication of hard words much enlarged this Eight Edition 1663.

The hard words now here Printed in this third Table, are many of them formerly Printed, for explaining the hard expressions in this Youths Behaviour, but many more newly added this year 1663, are taken either out of a Manuscript written 1620. The newer words not then usually spoken, are gathered out of Learned Authors. Printed for my self William Lee.

A

Aaron, a High-Priest, brother to Moses. Also of that name, was a great Emperour of the Saracens.
Abaddon, a destroyer.
Abyss, a bottomless pit.
Abjected, cast away, being vile, base, and good for nothing.
Abjudicated, given by judgement from one to another.
Abjuration, a denying or renouncing by Oath.
Ablution, a washing away.
Abolished, taken away.
Abortive, untimely born.
Abrogate, to undo or null a thing.
Abstracted, shortned, or one Book taken out of another.
Abstruse, hidden, secret, not easily understood.
Academy, a University, or great publick School.
Acceleration, a hastening.
† Accent, tune.
Accessary, which wittingly hideth an offender, or counselleth him in evil.
Accession, addition.
† Accommodate, to make fit, to apply.
Accost, to draw near to one.
Accumulate, to heap up.
† Accurately, cunningly done.
Acquiesce, to rest satisfied.
Acquire, to get or procure.
Acquitall, freeing one from an offence.

† Acre,

The third Table.

Acre, Land fourty pole in length, and four in breadth.
Acrimony, sharpness.
Acteoned, horned.
Action, a deed, or doing of a thing.
Actress, a woman-doer.
Acuminate, to whet or sharpen.
Adamant, diamond.
Adamatism, a loving dearly.
Adequate, to make levell.
Adfiliated, adopted for a son.
Adherent, which cleaveth to a thing.
Adjunct, one quality joyned to another, as heat to fire, &c.
Adjure, to bind by Oath.
Administer, to dispose of a dead mans goods.
Admirall, a great Officer at Sea, having the command of the Kings Name.
Adriatick Sea, the gulph of Venice.
Advent, the coming of certain weeks before Christmas.
Adverse, contrary, or against.
Adulation, flattery.
Advocate, one that pleadeth for another.
Adumbrated, shadowed forth.
Advowson, right of a Patron to present to a Spirituall benefice.
Adust, burnt.
Æstivate, to summer in a place.
Affable, courteous in speech.
Affect, to love.
Affectation, love of vain-glory.
Affiance, trust, confidence.
Affinity, kindred by marriage.
Affluence, plenty abundance.
Africa, the South part of the world.
Affrick-bird, a coward in fine cloathes.
Agast, amazed with fear, dismayed.
Agent, a helper in business.
Aggregate, to assemble together.
Aggravate, to make a fault worse and worse.
Agility, nimbleness.
Agitable, moveable.
Agitate, to toss, jogger shake.
Agnation, kindred by the fathers side.
Ajax's shield, a sure defence.
Aid, help.
Alacrity, chearfulness.
Alamode, after the French fashion.
Allayed, free from trouble, or sorrow vanisht away.
Almoner, an Officer in the Kings Court.
Alcaron, the Turks Law.
Allegation,

The third Table.

Allegation, proof of a matter.
Allegory, a dark sentence.
Alliance, league of friendship.
Alien, a stranger born, an outlandish man.
Aloes, a precious wood used in physick.
Altercation, an angry reasoning, or wrangling.
Altitude, height.
Amand, to send one away.
Amazonian, women belonging to Scythia, of manly courage.
Amber, a hard yellow gum whereof beads are made.
Ambergrease, the spawn of a whale, good for the brain.
Ambiguity, doubtfulness.
Ambrosia, (after the Poets) the meat of the Gods.
America, the West part of the world, found out by Americus Vespetius.
Amit, to send away.
Amort, dead.
Ample, great, or large.
Anagram, an invention, by altering the place of letters in ones Name.
Analysis, a resolution in doubtfull matters.
Anathematize, where the Church delivers over to the Devil.
Anallogy, correspondence, or proportion.

Anchorize, a religious woman living solitary.
Animadversion, a marking.
Animosity, heart-burning.
Anniversary, from year to year.
Annulet, a thing hung about the neck.
Annull, to make void.
Antagonist, enemy.
Antidote, a medicine against poison.
Antimony, a stone of a silver colour.
Antecedent, that which goeth before.
Antichrist, one against Christ.
Anticipate, to prevent or take before another.
Antipathy, a disagreement of qualities.
† Antiquate, to make old.
Anxiety, carefulness, sadness.
Aphorism, a short sentence expressing the properties of a thing.
Apoge, the point farthest from the center of the earth.
Apology, an excuse.
† Apoplexy, the dead palsey.
Apostasie, a falling from the faith.
Apostle, one sent as a messenger.
Apothegm, a quick short and witty sentence to note

Apparition

The third Table.

Apparition, *an appearing or vision.*
Appellation, *a calling or naming.*
† Appendix, *one thing that depends upon another.*
Appeal, *a removing a cause from an inferiour Court to a higher.*
† Apprehended, *taken by force.*
† Appropriation, *right to a thing.*
Arbitrator, *a Judge chosen to end controversies.*
Arbitrement, *an agreement made between two parties.*
Ardent, *vehement, burning hot.*
Argent, *silver, sometimes white.*
Aristocracy, *a government where the Nobility bear the sway.*
Arrogancy, *pride of heart.*
Arsenall, *a storehouse for armory or ships.*
Artick pole, *the North pole of the world.*
Artist, *one skilled in Arts.*
Aspect, *countenance.*
Asperate, *sharpness.*
† Aspiration, *a breathing.*
Assassinate, *to rob or murther privately in the high way.*
Assayer, *an Officer of the mint.*
Assent, *a yeelding, or agreeing to any thing.*

Assertion, *an affirming or avouching the truth of a thing.*
Assign, *to appoint.*
Assistance, *help.*
Assumpsit, *to undertake a thing for consideration.*
Astringent, *a binding.*
Atabulipa, *King of Peru in America.*
Atchievments, *things gained by valour.*
Atlantick Sea, *part of the mediterane Sea.*
Atome, *a small thing that cannot be made less.*
Attonement, *quietness.*
Attach, *to lay hands on.*
Attainted, *convicted, found guilty.*
Attempt, *to try, and endeavour.*
Attestation, *a witnessing.*
Attribute, *to bestow, or give.*
Attributes, *properties belonging to one.*
† Attrition, *repentance, or sorrow.*
Attorney, *he that by consent, taketh charge of another mans business.*
Audacity, *boldness, courage.*
Auditor, *an Officer of accounts.*
Aversion, *a disliking, a turning away.*
Auricular, *spoken in the ear.*
Aurora, *the morning.*
Axiome, *a maxime or sentence*

The third Table.

tence allowed to be true.
Aye, *for ever.*
Azur, *a fine blew colour.*
Azyme, *unleavened, unmingled.*

B

Balm, *a medicine for a green wound.*
Banded, *gathered into a faction.*
Baptize, *to wash.*
Barbarism, *rudeness in speech or behaviour, outragious cruelty.*
Baudes, *ancient Poets.*
Beatitude, *blessedness, or happiness.*
Belial, *signifying a wicked naughty person.*
Bellitude, *fairness.*
Benevolent, *loving or friendly.*
Benign, *gentle, courteous.*
Bequeathed, *left as a Legacy.*
Bereft, *deprived of.*
Berry, *a dwelling house. A Lord of a Mannor's Court.*
Besyen, *trouble.*
Betroth, *to make sure, to promise one in marriage.*
Bibacity, *immoderate love of drink.*
Bibliopolist, *a Bookseller.*
Bifront, *having two foreheads.*
Bissextile, *leap year, which is every fourth year.*
Blankers, *white furniture.*
Burrough, *not a City, but a Town incorporate.*

Brigade, *a body of souldiers.*
Brittain, *containing England and Scotland.*
Bucephalus, *Alexander's great horse.*
Buzzard, *a great Hawk, or Kite.*

C

Calculated, *reckoned or cast up.*
Caleb, *a Batchelor.*
Califie, *to warm.*
Calocity, *hardness.*
Calvary, *a place for dead mens bones.*
Calumniate, *falsly to accuse.*
Candidly, *meekly.*
Canon, *a Law.*
Canonize, *to pronounce one a Saint.*
Cantation, *singing.*
Captive, *led away prisoner.*
Caroll, *a song.*
Carpe, *to check or rebuke.*
Castrated, *gelded.*
Cavern, *a cave in the earth.*
Caveat, *a warning.*
Cautious, *wary.*
Caxicate, *indispose.*
Celebrate, *to do a thing in honour of him.*
Cement, *morter, lime.*
Censure, *opinion, judgement.*
Certificate, *a writing, averring the truth.*
Ceruse, *white lead.*
Chancellour, *a chief Officer in a principall Court.*
Character, *the form of a letter*

Charter,

The third Table.

Charter, *a writing of priviledges.*
Charmez, *a grain dying scarlet.*
Chivalry, *knighthood.*
Circumlocution, *over-speaking.*
Clandestine, *close, secret.*
Clarity, *nobleness, clearness.*
Clause, *a short sentence.*
Clemency, *gentleness.*
Cleopatra, *an Ægyptian Queen.*
Climate, *a portion between north and south.*
Clinches, *conceits.*
Coaction, *constraint.*
Coadjutor, *a fellow-helper.*
Coagulate, *to turn to a curd.*
Coasting, *a sailing from one coast to another.*
Coercive, *compelling.*
Coessential, *of the same essence or substance.*
Cognizance, *a hearing a thing judicially.*
Collacrimate, *to weep with.*
Colon, *a mark at a sentence not fully ended, as this (:)*
Comma, *a mark made thus (,) in writing*
Commemorate, *to rehearse, or make mention of.*
Commence, *to enter an action.*
Complacency, *agreableness.*
Compact, *agreement, a bargain.*
Compeers, *companions.*

Compendium, *a short way, a brief method.*
Comport, *to compose the gesture.*
Compunction, *grief, or remorse.*
Concise, *brief, short.*
Conclave, *private rooms, parlor, or closet.*
Concordance, *agreement.*
Congratulate, *to rejoyce in anothers behalf.*
Congruous, *agreeable.*
Conjugal, *belonging to wedlock.*
Connive, *to wink at.*
Connex, *to knit together*
Consanguinity, *kin by blood.*
Constitute, *to appoint or ordain.*
Consull, *a chief officer at Rome.*
Contemplation, *a pondering and thinking upon.*
Contingent, *casual, by chance.*
Contract, *bargain.*
Contribute, *to give with others.*
Contumacy, *stubborness, disobedience.*
Contumely, *disgrace, reproach.*
Convent, *to bring one before the Judg.*
Conversion, *a turning from evil to good.*
Convicted, *found guilty.*
Convocate, *to call together.*

Cooke,

The third Table.

Cooke, *a learned Lawyer, meant S. Edward Cooke, Lord Chief Justice of England in King James his time.*
Cooperate, *to work together.*
Corporation, *a body-politick.*
Corrigable, *which may be corrected.*
Corode, *to gnaw asunder.*
Creditor, *which lendeth, or trusteth money or wares.*
Credulity, *easiness of belief.*
Crevet, *a piece of fine linnen worn about the necks of Seamen, and now by Gentlemen riding.*
Cressent, *termed in Heraldry, the figure of a half Moon.*
Crispe, *curled.*
Critick, *a hard censurer.*
Cubit, *a measure from the elbow, to the end of the finger.*
Culpable, *faulty, blameable.*
Cupidity, *desire, covetousness.*
Cymicall, *doggish.*
Cyren, *Mermaids.*
Cyrus, *King of Persia.*

D

Debelitate, *to weaken.*
Decad, *the number of ten.*
Decipher, *to find out the meaning of a thing strangely written.*
Decision, *end of a matter in controversie.*
Declaime, *to speak ill of.*
Decoct, *to boyl, to seeth.*

Decretals, *Ordinances Decrees.*
Deduct, *to take away, or abate.*
Defatigate, *to make weary.*
Default, *an omitting what we ought to do.*
Define, *to declare, or describe.*
Defunct, *dead.*
Degenerate, *to turn out of kind.*
Degrade, *to take away holy orders.*
Dehort, *to disswade to the contrary.*
Delacrimate, *to weep.*
Delectation, *delight.*
Delegate, *to Assign, or send in Commission.*
Delude, *to deceive.*
Demaine, *the Lords Mannor-house.*
Demeanour, *behaviour.*
Demise, *to give, or grant.*
Democracy, *a free state, a people ruling themselves.*
Denizen, *a stranger born made free by Letters Patent.*
Denounce, *to threaten, to give warning.*
Deplorable, *to be lamented.*
Deportment, *behaviour in carriage.*
Deposition, *an oath, or deposing from authority.*
Depraved, *corrupted.*
Depress, *to keep down.*

Deprivation,

The third Table.

Deprivation, *a loss of a thing.*
Derogate, *to impair, diminish, or take away.*
Defection, *a mowing or cutting off.*
Designe, *to appoint, or intend.*
Desipiate, *to wax foolish.*
Despicable, *despised, accounted as nothing.*
Detect, *to discover, or disclose.*
Deterred, *discouraged.*
Detract, *to slander, to speak ill of.*
Detriment, *loss, hindrance, harm.*
Devastation, *a wasting.*
Devest, *to uncloath.*
Devoir, *endeavour.*
Devolve, *to roule down.*
Devoted, *vowed, bounden.*
Dexterity, *nimbleness.*
Dexteriously, *quickly.*
Dialectical, *belonging to Logick.*
Dicker, *ten hides of leather.*
Dictate, *a thing given to write.*
Diffidence, *distrust.*
Diffuse, *spread abroad.*
Digested, *set in order.*
Digression, *a passing from one thing to another.*
Dimension, *true measuring the bigness of a thing.*
Diminutive, *little, small.*
Dire, *fierce, cruel, terrible.*
Disanul, *to disallow.*

Discipline, *instruction, learning.*
Disclaiming, *disowning.*
Disconsolate, *comfortless.*
Discuss, *to examine, debate.*
Disfranchized, *ones freedome lost.*
Disgust, *to dislike.*
Dislocation, *a displacing.*
Dismall, *grievous, terrible.*
Dismantle, *to uncloath, to unfurnish.*
Dissert, *to dispute in matters.*
Dissipate, *to scatter abroad.*
Dissonant, *disagreeing.*
Distillation, *liquors dropping or dissolving by degrees.*
Divert, *to turn aside.*
Docible, *apt to be taught.*
Doctrine, *instruction for edifying.*
Document, *lesson.*
Dogmatical, *which is held in some opinion.*
Dominicall, *belonging to the Lords day.*
Donary, *a gift.*
Doughtis, *strong.*
Dowager, *a widow Princess.*
Dregging, *a dusting with powder.*
Drollery, *jesting.*
Dubious, *doubtfull.*
Dulsed, *sweet.*
Duplicate, *double.*
Duration, *a long continuance.*
Durity, *hardness.*
Dusky, *obscure, dark.*
Dyspathy,

The third Table

spathy, evill passion or affection.
spepsie, ill digestion of meat in the stomack.

E

ony, black timber, good for many purposes, especially for looking-glasses.
iety, drunkenness.
ypse, the Sun being darked.
ogs, shepheards poems.
fice, a framing or building.
cacious, able, powerfull.
sion, a powring forth.
ession, a going out.
t, to cast out.
orate, laborious, taking reat pains.
ate, to lift up.
tuary, a medicine made ith syrups and powders.
gant, fine, neat.
ie, a mournfull song.
ution, utterance, eloence in speaking
elsh, to make beautifull.
lem, a picture, something be learned by it.
rion, a child in the omb, before it hath perff shape.
nuel, God with us.
, to send forth.
hasis, a plain signification of ones mind.
kade, to swe one.
pctories, certain kernel places in the body, by which the principal parts void their superfluities.
Enormities, crimes, or offences.
Enterlude, stage play.
Enthusiasmes, political fury.
Epact, a number to find the age of the Moon by.
Epah, a measure of ten pottles.
Ephy, a measure of five peck.
Ephod, a holy garment worn by the high Priest.
Epidemical, the plague, or other diseases.
Epilogue, the end of a play.
Epithalmy, marriage-triumphs.
Epithete, an addition, as excessive pride; also put for a proper name, either of praising or dispraising.
Equinoctial line, the Sun coming twice a year, the 11th of March, and the 11th of Septemb. maketh the length of the dayes and nights equal.
Equipage, fashion.
Equivalent, of equal value.
Erudition, learning.
Eruption, a violent breaking out.
Escheater, an officer in the Exchequer, that certifieth what belongs to the King.
Essence, the substance of a thing.

Essoyne,

The third Table.

Essoyne, when a man by leave may absent himself from a Court.
Estreate, a coppy taken of any writing.
Etherial, belonging to the heavenly sphears.
Etimology, a true exposition of words.
Evacuate, to empty.
Evaporation, smoak or vapours.
Eversion, an overthrowing.
Evitable, all to be avoided.
Evoke, to call forth.
Exagerate, to encrease or amplifie a matter.
Exaltation, a lifting.
Exanimate, to amaze, to dishearten.
Excommunicate, to thrust one out of an Assembly.
Excrescency, a win swelling, or such like superfluities growing forth of the body.
Exemplifie, to declare a thing at large, to alleadge example.
Exempt, free from any payment.
Exercitation, use, practice.
Exhaile, to cast out a breath or fume.
Exhibit, to give, to present.
Exhilirate, to make merry.
Exigent, a streight, a hard pinch.
Exodus, a going out.

Exordium, a beginning.
Exodium, the end of a matter.
Exorbitances, things above order, rule, or measure.
Exonorate, to unburthen.
Expatiate, to enwiden, to enlarge.
Explication, the unfolding, or discovering of a thing.
Extenuate, to diminish or lessen.
Extraction, a drawing out, also a descending from such or such a family.
Extrinsecal, outward, or on the outside.
Extruded, thrust out.
Exult, to rejoyce.
Exundation, an over-flowing.
Exuperation, an excelling or surpassing.
Exustion, a burning.
Eyebite, to bewitch by the eye.
Ezekiel, the Prophet, signifieth, seeing the Lord.

F

Fabulous, false, as a lye.
Facetious, very pleasant.
Facil, easie.
Factious, troublesome, contentious.
Facilitate, to make easie.
Faculty, power, ability.
Facundity, eloquence.
Fallacious, deceitfull.
Fanatick, mad, lunatick, frantick, having vain apparitions.
Farce,

The third Table.

Farce, to stuff.
Fascination, an eye biting, or bewitching by the eye, or by the force of imagination.
Fate, destiny, chance.
Fatigate, to make weary.
Fealty, an oath taken of Tenants, to be true to their Lord.
Feaver-hecktick, that burns one inwardly, and makes cold without.
Fecundity, fruitfulness.
Fell, a skin
Fenchmonth, a month wherein Does do faun.
Feoffment, a gift, or grant of any honours.
Feracity, plenty, and abundance.
Ferocity, fierceness.
Fervent, hot.
Fiction, a feigning, or invention.
Figment, a lye.
Figurative, which serveth for the representation of another thing.
Flux, an issue of blood.
Fomentation, asswaging.
Foppery, foolery.
Forestall, to set afore anothers shop, or stall, to hinder light.
Formality, an observing of good order.
Formidable, cruel, fearfull to look on.
Fortitude, strength.
Foster, to cherish.
Fraction, a breaking off.
Fraturnity, brother hood.
Frication, rubbing, or chafing.
Frigidity, coldness.
Future, things to come.

G

Gabbing, lying.
Galen, a famous Physician.
Gambagas, large leather cases, or stirrops to keep the legs clean in riding.
Garbe, custome, or fashion.
Garboyle, a great rude noise.
Gargarisme, a liquer to wash ones mouth.
Gehenna, hell.
Generosity, courage, nobleness of mind.
Genitals, the privy members of any living creature.
Genius, a good or bad Angel, the soul.
Gentiles, all that are not converted to Christ.
Geomancy, divination by circles in the earth.
Germanity, brotherhood.
Gests, noble acts, commonly of Princes.
Geules, a red virmilion colour.
Glee, mirth, joyfulness.
Gloss, a short exposition of dark sentences.
Golden number, a number to find out the feast of Easter.
Golgotha, a place of skulls.
Gordion knot, a knot that cannot

cannot be undone.

Graduate, *one that takes his degree in the University.*

Gratuity, *a gift given freely, a reward.*

Gratulate, *to shew ones joy in anothers felicity.*

Graunge, *a village, a farme, a lone house in the countrey.*

Gubernate, *to govern.*

Guerdeon, *a reward.*

Gynophilus, *a lover of women.*

Gypsation, *a plaistering with morter.*

Gyration, *fetching a great compass.*

Gysarme, *a weapon with two pikes at the end.*

H

Haberdupoise, *a weight of sixteen ounces.*

Hability, *handsomness.*

Hags, *spirits of hell.*

Hamlet, *a village in the countrey.*

Harmony, *delightfull musick of many notes.*

Haubergeon, *a coat of male.*

Heben, *dull, blunt.*

Hecatombe, *a sacrifice wherein were offered a hundred beasts.*

Helvean-wine, *claret wine.*

Henchman, *a page of honour attending on a Prince.*

Hent, *to catch, or lay hold on.*

Herbage, *pasture for cattle.*

Hercules, *the son of Jupiter, a man famous for strength, he slew the Dragon, and got the golden apples.*

Heryos, *great, noble men.*

Hesper, *the evening star.*

Hesperides, *the garden where Hercules won the apples.*

Hests, *commands, or decrees.*

Heterodox, *a contrary opinion to what is generally received.*

Hexameter, *a verse of six feet.*

Hide of Land, *seven hundred acres.*

Hierarchy, *the holy order of Angels.*

Hieroglyphick, *a misticall represetation properly by sculpture.*

Hillarity, *mirth.*

Hippocrates, *a famous Physician.*

Homer, *a Grecian Poet.*

Humanity, *the nature and condition of mar; also gentleness, mildness.*

Hydrography, *description of waters.*

Hyperbolicall, *above all belief, as swifter than thought.*

Hysteron & proteron, *cart before the horse.*

I

Jaculation, *a darting, casting of darts.*

Idea, *the form of any thing conceived in the mind.*

Idea,

The third Table.

Ides, *eight dayes in every moneth.*
Jeopardy, *hazard.*
Ignominious, *shamefull.*
Iliads, *a book writ in Greek by Homer, of the destruction of Troy.*
Illiberal, *covetous, base.*
Illustrate, *to make famous.*
Imagery, *carving, or painting.*
Imbellishments, *ornaments.*
Imbroile, *to make more obscure.*
Imbrued, *stained.*
Immaculate, *undefiled.*
Immence, *unmeasured.*
Immunity, *freedom, liberty.*
Immutable, *constant, unchangeable.*
Impaire, *to lessen.*
Imparadized, *to enjoy all true contentment.*
Imparity, *unlikenefs.*
Impeach, *to hinder, to harm.*
Impenfible, *without reward.*
Impetuous, *violent.*
Implore, *humbly to request.*
Impoft, *custome.*
Imprecations, *cursings.*
Improperations, *reproachings.*
Impropriation, *Ecclesiastical living, coming by inheritance.*
Impugne, *to resist, or assault.*
Impunity, *lack of punishment.*
Incendiary, *which setteth any thing on fire.*
Inclusive, *which containeth.*
Incongruous, *absurd, disagreeable.*
Incorporeal, *having no body.*
Incorrigable, *that cannot be amended.*
Inculcate, *to repeat a thing often.*
Inculpable, *blameless.*
Incursion, *a running in a meeting together.*
Indefatigable, *not to be tired.*
Indefinite, *obscure, not determined.*
Indempnity, *pardon, escaping without punishment.*
Indeprecable, *that will not be entreated.*
Indigent, *needy, beggarly.*
Indignity, *unworthinefs.*
Individual, *not to be parted as man and wife.*
Indocible, *which cannot be taught.*
Induce, *to bring in.*
Indulgence, *gentlenefs in suffering.*
Indurate, *to harden.*
Ineffable, *not to be spoken.*
Inexpiable, *which cannot be satisfied for.*
Infamy, *difgrace.*
Infatigable, *that cannot be wearied.*
Infatuate, *to besot.*

Inferre,

The third Table.

Inferre, *to bring in by way of argument.*
Infestuous, *noisome.*
Infirme, *weak.*
Inflammation, *a hot angry swelling.*
Inflect, *to bow, or make crooked.*
Influence, *a flowing power of Planets and Stars.*
Infrenge, *to break.*
Ingots, *a wedge of fine gold.*
Inhibit, *to forbid.*
Inherent, *abiding in a thing.*
Inhospitable, *not fit for entertainment.*
Innate, *natural.*
Innavigable, *not to be sailed in.*
Innominable, *not to be named.*
Innovations, *changes.*
Inoculate, *to graff.*
Insanable, *not to be cured.*
Inscrutable, *not to be searched.*
Insculp, *to ingrave, or cut.*
Insection, *a declaration, or long continuance.*
Insociable, *not fit to keep any company.*
Inspection, *a looking into.*
Insinuation, *a cunning speech to get into ones favour.*
Inspire, *to breath into.*
Instauration, *a repairing.*
Instigate, *to provoke.*
Instinct, *a natural inclination.*

Institute, *to appoint.*
Insult, *to boast proudly.*
Intactable, *not to be touched.*
Intaminate, *to defile.*
Integration, *a restoring.*
Integrity, *uprightness, just dealing.*
Intellects, *the understanding, and other faculties of the mind.*
Intemperance, *unruly, immoderate eating or drinking.*
Intercession, *an entreaty in ones behalf.*
Intercourse, *passing, or sending from one to another.*
Interdict, *to forbid.*
Interest, *right, or title, profit made by usury.*
Interior, *inward.*
Interlocution, *a speaking between.*
Interlude, *a pastime or play.*
Interpose, *to busie himself where he need not.*
Interrex, *he that governs when there is no King.*
Interrogation, *the asking of a question.*
Interview, *meeting.*
Intestine, *bred in the bowels.*
Intimation, *a cunning signifying.*
Intoxicated, *to bewitch, to poyson.*
Intrinsecal, *inward.*
Introduct, *to lead in.*
Intumulated

The third Table.

Intumulated, *not buried.*
Invalidity, *weakness.*
Inveloped, *wrapped in.*
Inversion, *a turning up-side down.*
Invest, *to cloath.*
Inumbrate, *to cast a shadow.*
Invocation, *a calling upon.*
Inured, *accustomed to.*
Joculatory, *merrily spoken.*
Jovinus, *a famous historian.*
Ironycally, *spoken scoffingly.*
Irradiate, *to shine upon.*
Irregular, *contrary to rule.*
Irrevocable, *not to be called back.*
Irrogate, *to impose.*
Itinerate, *to journey.*
Judra, *jury.*
Juditious, *one that hath great judgment.*
Julius Cæsar, *a famous Roman, the first Emperour of Rome.*
Juncture, *a joyning together.*
Juror, *a swearer.*
Jurisdiction, *a lawfull authority.*
Juvenility, *youth.*

K

Keele, *the bottome of a ship.*
Kenne, *to view.*
Kintall, *a hundred weight.*
Knightservice, *a tenure where a man was bound to bear arms for the defence of the Realm.*
Knight, *a title of dignity and honour; which word is illustrated with divers distinctions, viz. Knights Batchelours, Knights Bannerets, Knights Barronets, Knights of the Bath, Knights of the Carpet, Knights of the Garter, Knights of the Order of St. John of Jerusalem, Knights Templers, or Knights of the Temple, Knights of the Shire, Knights Marshall, Knights of Calatrava in Spain, Knights of the Star.*
Kyrie Eleison, *in the Greek, Lord have mercy upon us.*

L

Lacerate, *to tear.*
Lacrimate, *to lament, to cry.*
Landskip, *a piece of painting, wherein are woods, rocks, houses, rivers, or the skye painted.*
Latitude, *the breadth of a thing.*
Laurii, *the bay tree.*
Leconomony, *divination by water in a bason.*
Legat, *the Popes Ambassadors.*
Legion, *of horse and foot, 6826.*
Legislator, *a law-maker, or giver.*
Lemma, *argument.*
Leniment, *an assuaging.*

Lenity,

The third Table.

Lenity, gentleness.
Lenitude, slowness, negligence.
Lesse, he that taketh a lease.
Lessor, he that letteth.
Levity, lightness.
Libertine, one of a loose life.
Libidinous, incontinent, full of lustfull desires.
Lineament, the proportion of the body.
Linial, downright line.
Liquation, a melting.
Literate, learned.
Liturgy, the publick Service of the Church.
Local, of, or belonging to a place.
Locust, grashoppers, and such like vermine.
Logick, the art of reason.
Longuanimity, patience, long-suffering.
Loquacity, much talk and babling.
Lorrel, a devourer.
Lossel, a crafty fellow, a lout.
Lotion, a washing.
Lubrick, slippery.
Lucible, that which is light of it self.
Lucifer, the morning star, also an Arch-Devil.
Lucrece, a Romane dame, who being ravished killed her self.
Lurcate, to eat ravenously.
Luxury, riot, wantonness.
Library, a study of Books, or a place where Books are kept.
Lydford Law, whereby first a man is hanged, and afterward indited.
Lyrick, verses, or songs upon the harp.

M

Macrate, to soak in water, to make clean.
Macrology, long, or tedious talk.
Maculate, to spot, or blemish.
Magick, enchantment, sorcery.
Magnanimity, boldness, nobleness of heart.
Magnificence, honour, statelyness.
Mainprize, the bailing one out of prison, security for his forth-coming.
Malediction, cursing, ill speaking.
Malignant, envious, spitefull.
Mandare, to command.
Manna, white, much like Coliander seed.
Mansion, a dwelling house.
Marches, bounds, lying between two countries.
Maritane, bordering on the Sea.
Mars, the heathen god of battle.
Masculine, manlike.
Mature, ripe.
Maugre, in despight of ones heart.
Maxime, a true and generall rule.

Mean-

The third Table.

Meanders, crooked turnings.
Mechanism, the learning of handy-craft trades.
Mediocrity, a mean, or measure.
Meliocrity, a bettering.
Memorandum, to remember us of that which we would not forget.
Memorize, to recount.
Mendicant, begging.
Meridian, of or belonging to noon-tide.
Merit, desert.
Messalina, an Empress of Rome, an unsatiable woman
Messias, annoynted.
Metaphor, one word taken for another.
Metaphysicks, supernaturall Arts.
Meteor, snow, hail, thunder.
Method, a direct way to teach
Mimick, a scoffer, or jester.
Menace, to threaten.
Miscreant, an infidel.
Misprise, to have a low esteem.
Mission, a sending.
Mode, fashion.
Modern, living now in our age
Moloch, an idol like a Calf.
Monology, a long tale of little worth.
Morall, appertaining to civility, or good manners.
Morosity, waywardness, frowardness.
Motto, a short sentence, a word

Mounsieur, in french, good Sir.
Mountebank, one that boasteth on high of his great deeds, deceiving the people.
Mulct, a fine, or penalty.
Mummy, a thing like pitch, the fat of dead men kept by Apothecaries.
Munificence, liberality.
Municipall, priviledges of Laws belonging to Cities.
Mutiny, a quarrell among souldiers.
Mutuall, interchangeable.
Mysticall, hidden, secret.

N

Napar, fine linen for the table
Narration, a declaring.
Nectar, the drink of the gods.
Negotiation, business in traffick and trade.
Nepenthe, an herb that expells sadness.
Nero, an Emperour of Rome, a cruell man.
Ninny, a fool.
Nocent, hurtfull.
Non-residence, unlawfull absence from the place of ones abode.
Non-suit, the letting fall of a Suit.
Novelty, news.
Nulli fidian, of no account, or religion.
Nusceous, purblind.
Nusance, any annoyance, or damage done to a house.
Nutriment, nourishment.

H 4   Obfuscate,

O

Obfuscate, *to cloud, or darken.*
Objure, *to bind by Oath.*
Objurgation, *a chiding.*
Oblique, *crooked.*
Obligurate, *to spend in belly chear.*
Obliterate, *to blot out.*
Obnoxious, *subject to danger.*
Obsequious, *dutifull.*
Obsolete, *old, out of use.*
Obstruct, *to hinder.*
Obtrude, *to thrust out.*
Obtuse, *dull, or blunt.*
Obumbrate, *to shadow.*
Occur, *to meet.*
Oeconomy, *government of a houshold.*
Officious, *serviceable, willing to please.*
Olympick games, *solemn games of activity.*
Omission, *a letting slip.*
Oppilation, *stopping.*
Opponent, *which opposeth, or asketh questions.*
Opprobrious, *reproachfull.*
Oppugn, *to resist.*
Opulent, *rich, wealthy.*
Ore, *gold or silver colour.*
Ordinary, *a Judge having jurisdiction in Church-matters.*
Orient, *the East.*
Orifice, *the mouth of a wound, or any other thing.*
Orisons, *prayers.*
Orphan, *one that wants father and mother.*
Orthodox, *learned, of a sound judgement, or right opinion.*
Osier, *a Withy.*
Ostentation, *a boasting.*
Overture, *an over-turning, a sudden change.*
Ounce, *being the sixteenth part of a pound.*
Oyer and terminer, *a Commission to hear and determine causes.*

P

Pact, *a bargain.*
Pagan, *one that doth not believe in God.*
Palliate, *to cloake, to cover.*
Palm, *the tree that bears dates.*
Pandect, *a book treating of all matters.*
Panick, *fear.*
Pantaloon, *a large boothose top.*
Paradise, *a garden, or pleasant place.*
Paragon, *a beautifull Lady.*
Parallels, *lines at an equall distance, or the comparing one thing with another.*
Paramour, *a sweet-heart.*
Paramount, *the chief Lord of a See.*
Parasite, *a flatterer, or trencher friend.*
Parity, *likeness.*
Parsimony,

Parsimony, *thriftiness, good husbandry.*
Participate, *to partake, or have a share in a thing.*
Partison, *a weapon like a halbert.*
Parvity, *smalness.*
Pasche, *the feast of Easter.*
Pastor, *shepherd.*
Paternall, *belonging to a father.*
Patheticall, *moving love.*
Patriarch, *a chief father of the Church.*
Patrimony, *goods, or lands left by friends.*
Pavilion, *a tent for war.*
Peccant, *faulty.*
Pedantick, *a base ignorant fellow.*
Pendent, *hanging downward.*
Penelope, *a chast woman.*
Perforations, *little passages.*
Periwix, *false hair.*
Perpetuity, *everlasting.*
Perspicuous, *clear.*
Pervert, *to turn one from good to bad.*
Pestiforous, *mortall, deadly.*
Pettifogger, *a troublesome makebate, ignorant medler in Law.*
Petulant, *sawcy.*
Phantasm, *a vision, or imagined appearance.*
Pharisee, *a sort of Jews, professing more holiness than the common sort.*
Philomathy, *the love of learning.*
Phlebotomy, *blood-letting.*
Phantasticall, *foolish, following every fashion.*
Placability, *gentleness.*
Plato, *a famous Philosopher.*
Plausible, *that which greatly pleaseth.*
Plebean, *one of the common people.*
Plenary, *full, entire.*
Plumbeous, *full of lead, heavy.*
Pocahuncas, *daughter to a savage King of* Virginia.
Poetaster, *a counterfeit Poet.*
Poligamy, *the having of many wives.*
Poppæa Sabina, *wife to* Nero.
Popular, *favour with the common people.*
Portage, *carriage.*
Portend, *to fore-show a thing.*
Positive, *that which is propounded.*
Posthume, *born after his fathers death.*
Pravity, *naughty, wicked.*
Precaution, *wariness, forewarning.*
Precipitate, *to throw down headlong.*
Precontract, *a former bargain.*
Predicament, *a different order in the nature of things.* Predicate,

The third Table.

Predicate, *to foretell.*
Prefect, *a chief Magistrate.*
Pregnant, *witty, apt, forward: or great with child.*
Prejudicate, *to judge rashly.*
Premunire, *a punishment wherein is loss of goods and liberty during life.*
Presuse, *foreskin.*
Presage, *foretell.*
Presbitery, *priesthood.*
Prescience, *a knowing before.*
Pressure, *an oppression.*
Pretext, *a colourable excuse.*
Prevalency, *prevailing.*
Prigg, *to steal.*
Prodigious, *monstrous.*
Product, *brought forth.*
Progenitors, *ancestors.*
Prolix, *long, or tedious.*
Prolocutor, *one that speaks first, or for the rest, a speaker.*
Propagate, *to spread abroad.*
Propinquity, *nearness.*
Propitiation, *an appeasing of Gods anger.*
Propose, *to offer, to set forth.*
Proselyte, *a stranger converted.*
Prosodie, *the true pronouncing of words.*
Providence, *foresight, care.*
Proviso, *a condition made in any writing.*

Prowess, *strength, courage.*
Pseudomartyr, *a false martyr.*
Puberty, *ripeness, fourteen in men, and twelve in women.*
Pudor, *shamefastness.*
Pularity, *girlishness.*
Punctuall, *one as good as his word.*
Purgatory, *a place of purging.*
Purport, *an intent or meaning.*
Pusill, *small.*
Pustule, *a wheal, or blister.*
Putrid, *corrupt.*
Pythagoras, *a famous Philosopher, the chief that held the passing of souls out of one body into another.*
Polemicall, *military, belonging to war.*

Q

Quadrant, *four-square.*
Quaint, *fine stranger.*
Quest, *a search, an enquiry.*
Quiddities, *subtill, dark speeches.*

R

Rabbi, *master, or Doctor.*
Rabbine, *a great Doctor or teacher.*
Radiant, *bright, shining.*
Radicall, *of or belonging to the root.*
Rarifie, *to make thin.*
Ratification, *a confirmation, or allowing.* Reassume,

The third Table.

Reassume, *to take again.*
Recapitulate, *to relate in brief.*
Reciprocal, *of, or belonging to returning.*
Recognizance, *an acknowledgment.*
Recruit, *to recover ones self.*
Recusant, *which refuseth to do a thing.*
Redundancy, *an overflowing, abounding, or exceeding.*
Refell, *to disprove.*
Refined, *purified.*
Reflection, *a bowing, or bending back.*
Refulgent, *bright, shining.*
Refund, *restore.*
Regality, *authority of a King.*
Regrator, *he that buyeth victuals to sell within four miles.*
Regress, *going back.*
Rejoynder, *a second answer.*
Remit, *to forgive, also to send back.*
Remonstrance, *reasons given or shewed.*
Remunarate, *reward.*
Republick, *Commonwealth.*
Repugne, *to resist.*
Resentment, *sensible of a disfavour or injury.*
Result, *to keep back.*
Retaliate, *to quit like for like.*
Retract, *to call back.*
Retribution, *a reward or recompence.*
Retrive, *to seek again.*
Retrograde, *backward.*
Revert, *to return.*
Rigid, *hard, stubborne.*
Risco, *great hazard, or danger.*
Robustious, *strong.*
Rubrick, *order, or rule written.*
Rurall, *of, or belonging to the country.*
Rustication, *a dwelling in the country.*

Sabboth, *day of rest.*
Sagacity, *swiftness, quickness of understand, or sharpness of wit.*
Sally-ports, *the back or postern gates, gates to issue out of a fort or bulwark.*
Satiety, *fulness.*
Satyr, *a wild god of the woods.*
Skeleton, *the bones of a man without flesh or skin.*
Schismatical, *erroneous.*
Scholastical, *learned.*
Secular, *worldly.*
Sedulity, *diligence.*
Seneca, *a stoick Philosopher.*
Sewer, *one that placeth the meat at table.*
Sewers, *common channels.*
Signal, *a sign, or note.*
Sin, *derogating, or erring from the truth.*
Sinister, *unhappy, harmfull.*
Solecisme, *a false manner of speaking*

The third Table.

Solicitous, *carefull.*
Sophister, *a subtile caviler in words.*
Sordid, *base, filthy.*
Species, *the different kind of a thing.*
Speculation, *a beholding.*
Sphere, *a round circle.*
Spleen, *the milt of man or beast.*
Stanaries, *mines of tin.*
Steed, *a lusty horse.*
Steril, *barren.*
Stigmatical, *a lewd liver.*
Stupid, *dull, blockish.*
Sublime, *high and lofty.*
Subordinate, *under another.*
Subsidy, *aid, or succour.*
Subvert, *to overthrow.*
Sulpher, *brimstone.*
Summary, *brief.*
Superficies, *the outside of a thing.*
Superlative, *highest.*
Supersedeas, *forbidding.*
Surplussage, *more than needs.*
Surrogate, *to substitute.*
Swaine, *a servant.*
Sycophant, *a tale-bearer, a slanderer.*
Sympathize, *mutually to embrace each other.*
Symptomes, *grief, following a disease; also signes whereby to discover the nature of a disease.*
Syntax, *a joyning together of parts of speech in one construction.*

T

Tabernacle, *a tent, or pavillion.*
Taciturnity, *silence.*
Tallent, *a thing given to improve.*
Tallage, *fraught or custome.*
Tardy, *slow.*
Tarquin, *last King of Rome.*
Tautology, *often repeating a sentence.*
Tenebrous, *dark.*
Tergiversation, *seeming to run away, but stand to it wrangling.*
Terminate, *to end.*
Testator, *he that maketh a will.*
Tetragammanton, *the great name of God.*
Tetarch, *a Prince ruling a fourth part of a Kingdome.*
Theorick, *study, the inward knowledg of a thing.*
Thrall, *bondage, misery.*
Tinctures, *spots or stains in dying.*
Tirulation, *a tickling.*
Torrent, *hot.*
Tranquility, *ease, quietness of mind.*
Transmute, *to change.*
Transpiration, *breathing out the vapours.*
Traverse, *to go across, or overthwart.*
Trepan, *betray.*
Tripartite, *threefold.*

Triviall,

iviall, *base, vile, of no esti-mation.*
oy weight, *twelve ounces.*
rpid, *filthy.*
ype, *the figure, or shadow of a thing.*
rociny, *an apprentiship, a beginning in the military discipline.*

U

cuity, *emptiness.*
unt, *to brag, or boast.*
getivals, *belonging to plants.*
le, *a covering for women.*
nerable, *worshipfull.*
nial, *easily pardoned.*
nus, *one of the seven stars, also the goddess of lust or lentry.*
sed, *very perfect in.*
sion, *a turning.*
r, *green.*
inity, *neighbourhood.*
issitude, *change.*
, *to dare or threaten.*
lancy, *watchfullness.*
lity, *manhood.*
icity, *liveliness, long life.*
verse, *the whole.*
iferation, *a loud voice.*
iminous, *a great book, or a an having great volumes.*
, *learning.*
sil, *necessary houshold stuff.*
ty, *profit.*
erate, *to wound or hurt.*
inate, *fox-like, to deceive.*
on, *a pulling.*

Uxorious, *doating upon a wife.*

W

Wanze, *to perish, to decay.*
Warison, *a reward.*
Welked, *withered.*
Welkin, *the whole sky.*
Wile, *deceit, craft.*
Wisdom, *the truth and reason of things, which all men should seek after.*
Wreck, *the loss of a ship at Sea.*
Writ, *the Kings Precept, for a distress to be taken.*

X

Xenodochy, *hospitality.*
Xenophon, *a famous Athenian Philosopher.*
Xerxes, *a King of Persia.*

Y

Yarrow, *faint-hearted, fearfull.*
Year, and day, *a construction commonly used in the common Law.*
Yeaman, *the next degree to a Livery, or Gentleman.*
Yexing, *sobing.*
Yonker, *a lusty lad.*
Yore, *long ago, of old.*

Z

Zelotophy, *jealousie.*
Zodiack, *a circle in the heavens, in which the twelve Planets are placed.*
Zone, *a belt or girdle.*
Zygost, *one appointed to look to weights, a Clerk of the Market.*

ERRATA

ERRATA

At the end of the

SECOND TABLE.

The Latine and English Verses, thus to be read.

> HAbet omnis hoc Voluptas,
> Stimulis agit furentes;
> Apiumque par volantûm
> Ubi grata mella fudit,
> Fugit, & nimis Tenaci
> Ferit Icta corda morsu.

All pleasures are but sad,
And in their end are mad; (flight
As the angry Bee, that which it's wandri
From fragrant flowers sipt, converts the spight
So pleasure leaves a grief within the brest,
Not to be cur'd, but by a blessed Rest.

A POST

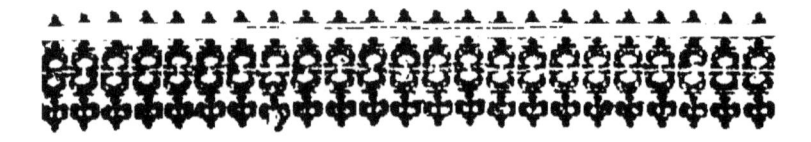

A POSTSCRIPT

Of some few words

Added and Explained.

A

Alternation, *a changing.*
Analogy, *proportion, correspondence.*
Anagoge, *a figure in Rhetorick.*
Assimulation, *a likening, a resembling.*
Augury, *southsaying, or divining by the flying of birds.*

D

Deprecation, *a diverting Gods judgments by prayer.*

G

Gladiator, *a swordman, or fencer.*

O

Obsequious, *diligent to please.*

S

Sanhedrim, *a great Counsel of the Jews.*
Scholiasts, *a Coment on a close or good Author.*
Source, *Spring or fountain.*
Sublunary, *things under the Moon.*

A Catalogue of some of the latest Books Printed for William Lee, and are to be sold at his Shop, at the Turks head in Fleetstreet.

A System, or, Body of Divinity, consisting of X Books; by Edward Leigh Esq; the second Edition, with about a hundred sheets added in the body of the Book, besides Additions at the end. Printed 1662. Price 18s Bound.

Silva Silvarum, or a Natural History, in ten Centuries, whereunto is added, the History of Life and Death, or the Prolongation of Life; by the Right Honourable Francis Bacon Baron of Verulam, in Fol. 1658. Price 5s in Quires.

Resucitatio, or bringing into publick light several pieces of the Works hitherto sleeping, of the Right Honourable Francis Lord Bacon, Baron of Verulam, together with his Lordships Life, not before published The second Edition inlarged. 1661. Price 7s in Quires.

The Triumphs of Gods Revenge against Murther, in Thirty Tragical Histories; digested into six Books, by John Reynolds. The fourth Edition, illustrated with Brass Plates. 1663. Price 8s in Quires.

Heresiography, or a Description of the Heresies and Sectaries of these latter times; the sixth Edition, by E. Pagit, much enlarged. 8o. With Vennors Treason. 1662. 2s Bound.

Dods 10 Sermons on the Lords Supper, with his Life, and two Epistles, and his Picture, 1661. Price 2s Bound.

Lathams Falconry, with many new Additions. 1661. Price 3s Bound.

Grotius of War and Peace, English, 8o large. Price 4s Bound.

—His two Treatises of God and his Providence, o Christ and his Miracles; with the Authors judgement o sundry Points controverted. 12o. Both translated by Clement Barksdale. Price 1s Bound.

The degrees of Marriage, allowed by the Lord Arch Bishop of Canterbury; the only true Coppy. 1662.

Imprimatur.

Ex Æd. Sab. Geo. Stradling, S.T.P. Reu. in Christ
Nov. 15. 1662. Pat. Gilb. Episc. Lond. à sac. domest.

FINIS.